WOOD & BRISTLE

WOOD & BRISTLE

Woodwork and Brushmaking Projects for Everyday Living

Sophia Elouise

Library of Congress Control Number: 2025939813

Produced by BlueRed Press Ltd., 2026
Designed by Insight Design Concepts Ltd.
Type set in Avenir and Ravensara Serif

Photo credits
All photos by the author except: Beech tree (mirkomedia), Sycamore Gap (Alan C Gordon), close-up of green and brown seeds of *Acer pseudoplatanus* or *Acer opalus* (Tanya), hanging hairy male flowers and young leaves on a branch of a beech tree (*Fagus sylvatica*) in spring (Maren Winter), hand saw and wood planks, saw with a Japanese tooth, and maple wood (Yura Borisov), backsaw with reinforced spine (OMD), Dozuki saws (Thomas Moens).
P. 26 (left): Roger Culos/WikiCommons CC BY-SA 4.0, P. 29 (bottom): Roger Culos/WikiCommons CC BY-SA 3.0, P. 27 (top): Bubba73 (Jud McCranie)/WikiCommons CC BY-SA 4.0, P. 27 (bottom): Famartin/ WikiCommons CC BY-SA 4.0, P28 (Top) - Superstock

ISBN: 978-0-7643-7134-9
Printed in China
10 9 8 7 6 5 4 3 2 1

Published by Schiffer Craft
An imprint of Schiffer Publishing, Ltd.
4880 Lower Valley Road
Atglen, PA 19310
Phone: (610) 593-1777; Fax: (610) 593-2002
Email: Info@schifferbooks.com
Web: www.schifferbooks.com

CONTENTS

INTRODUCTION

Working with natural materials always grounds me. Maybe it takes me back to being a child, climbing trees, crawling through long grass, and letting my imagination run wild. Whatever it is, it captivates me and is a meditative process that takes me out of my brain and into my body. These days, we understand more and more as a society about the importance of natural materials in our homes, around our bodies, and in our environments. In reality, this takes us full circle back to where we began, utilizing the materials in our environments to create the tools we need to live.

It can be hard to find natural materials in your home that haven't been somehow interfered with or added to, with either plastics, glues, or chemicals. Most of our "wooden" items in the home are now made from MDF (medium-density fiberboard) or plywood—two great alternatives. However, they contain a large amount of glue and other binding chemicals. If you were to walk around your home now, you could well discover that to find solid, untampered-with wood, you are left with only your banister (if you have stairs) and a wooden spoon. Although for manufacturers, this is a winner, for our health and mental well-being, this needs to be questioned. Research has proven that having natural materials in the home not only calms the mind and has a positive impact on mental health, but also dramatically helps with child development and learning. The durability and strength of natural materials mean we can use them for generations with minimal impact on our environment.

In this book I want to share with you a selection of projects and tools that will introduce or develop a set of skills for you to work with natural materials. These skills will be foundational in going forward and filling your home with tools and pieces that are not only completely natural and sustainable, but also created with your very own hands.

A Woman in Woodwork

I feel so fortunate to have had encouragement to do what I enjoyed. It began with my family, with parents who never gendered activities or discouraged me and my sisters from being "boisterous" and downright bizarre. It gave me space to grow into a confident woman, unafraid of walking into a timber yard full of men. I also need to give due credit to the brilliant, skillful teachers and mentors I have had encouraging me along the way, sharing time, tools, skills, and passion with me. Although in an ideal world, 50 percent of the woodworking workforce would be female, I am so grateful to those who did hire me, train me, and share their workshops with me, because—and they know this— another woman in the workshop is what young girls and boys deserve to see.

History suggests that women have, in fact, always been part of the woodworking workforce but have rarely been recognized for it. I actually believe that working with wood, fibers, and metals is an incredibly feminine impulse; it is to be in contact with the earth, familiar with the environment around us, and to nest ourselves in the world by understanding it in this way.

Although I trained in joinery and woodwork, my degree before this was in fine art, where I worked predominantly with materials such as stone and metal. Now I find that I have come full circle back to this, and in my current work I use metals, plant fibers, and textiles. Furthermore, I have stone-carving plans on the horizon—I can't help myself; the more natural the materials, the better! My work is a balance point between function and form, and I strive to create minimally elegant pieces that celebrate the beauty of the material without constraining them to simply display pieces. Each piece is designed with utility in mind since, I believe, daily use allows us to cherish an item for generations to come.

Function & Form is my sustainable practice business which upholds traditional techniques to create natural, utilitarian pieces for slow living. I design and create all pieces in small batches from my studio in North Yorkshire. Rooted in the belief that objects can be both sculptural and practical, it is the amalgamation of my training in fine art, sculpture, and joinery. You can purchase my work through my online shop as well as book tickets to workshops to learn traditional skills in person with me.

Website: www.function-and-form.com
Instagram: @function_and_form_
Email: sophia@function-and-form.com

My Background

"How did you get into woodworking then?" It's a question I get asked a lot. In truth, I don't think I ever seriously considered a way of life where I don't get to work with my hands and body. Growing up in my dad's sculpting workshop and with my mom—a textile artist—making our clothes, I was inundated with inspiration and keen to see where my own creativity would lead. The fourth of four children in the family, I took my turn through my late teens, working with Dad over summer vacations and soaking up the incredible skills and knowledge that he, and his workshop, had to offer.

After school, I went on to do a foundation in art and design at Leeds College of Art and then a BA in fine art at Falmouth University in Cornwall. During these years—aside from spending a lot of time in the sea—my creative practice played with all sorts of media, from performance work to building microphones from scratch in order to record sound pieces. However, I found my grounding space in the workshops, learning from the technicians, working to form natural materials in metal beating, stone carving, and woodwork.

After university I trained and worked with a joinery company in Wiltshire, creating beautiful furniture and sculptural works from English hardwoods. Although all the wood used was sustainably sourced and FSC (Forest Stewardship Council) approved, due to the nature of joinery work, there was waste product, which was painful to discard. I began collecting bits of "burn pile" wood that I saw beauty in and would use my spare time to create pieces from them. From this, my creative practice became my business, and I began creating utility-based pieces that could be used functionally to ensure the wood did not go to waste and could instead be cherished for lifetimes.

I was fortunate enough to be selected to be part of the Black Swan Art's Studios and Gallery spaces in Frome, Somerset, and this was my first time working in my own creative environment since Falmouth. I worked alongside some fantastic makers, all of whom I thoroughly enjoyed working (and going to pubs) with. During my first studio years I was excited for my work to be featured in *Country Living* and *Almanac Magazine*, as well as showcasing work in multiple different exhibitions and being selected for shows such as Bovey Tracey Craft Festival, various Royal Horticultural Society shows, and the Great Northern Contemporary Craft fairs. I am now in my second workshop after relocating back to my home county of North Yorkshire. From here I create all of my pieces as well as running workshops in different areas of woodworking, brushmaking, and general machinery and power tool skills. I run workshops for all ages, abilities, and interests and love to run my "Women in the Workshop" sessions, which specifically encourage those who identify as female to come and learn DIY and power tool skills in a comfortable environment.

Being a woman in a male-dominated industry has come with its challenges, but for every person who has felt the need to question my abilities, there have been ten more supporting me, sharing their knowledge, time, and tools. I have had some incredible teachers through the years in the form of parents, siblings, bosses, and friends who have given guidance and support, for which I am so incredibly grateful. My aim is to pay that knowledge and support forward with my own experience and, I hope, act as a reference for all who identify as female to get into the workshop, use the tools, and feel empowered.

FUNCTION & FORM

Sustainability and Natural Materials

Research has shown that natural materials around the home have a profound effect not only on our physical health, but on our mental health also. So many of us spend a lot more time in our homes than we did just a couple of years ago with the adjustment of remote working. An average person (not necessarily working from home) will spend approximately forty-eight years of their life in their home—about 60 percent of your lifetime. Putting this figure in perspective, it shows how important home environments are to our overall health and well-being.

Of course, unless you build a house from the ground up, you don't necessarily have a say in all the materials that go into your home, but in the areas you do have a say, it is important to try to find the materials that are in the closest to their natural form as possible. Natural materials do have a life of their own and a growth history, which means they don't always act as we would expect, but the trick is knowing how to care for these materials: In return, the materials care for you.

Sustainability and natural materials mostly go hand in hand. The materials I focus on in this book are all renewable, meaning they will regrow. The exception to this is use of metal for the wire-drawn setting—although metals can be recycled indefinitely with little impact on quality. Challenges to sustainability and natural materials occur when materials are not harvested properly; for example, when timber is cut from forests without sustainable procedures in place to protect the biodiversity of the forest and the people around it.

Here are a few bullet points to consider while trying to source natural materials sustainably:

Biodegradability

This is a big one—is the material able to be broken down by microbes and feed nutrients back into the soil once you have finished with it? Natural wood, plant fibers, and natural cord can do this, but sometimes it's also important to look at the finishes or dyes on these products, since some of these processes can't be broken down in the soil.

Growth

Think about or do some research on the growth process of the plant or ground that your material comes from—does it take a lot of water and nutrients to grow? Look for fibers like the ones we use in this book that require minimal water and mineral usage to grow and grow rapidly; these kinds of materials make fewer demands of the soil and environment they grow in.

Proximity

There are many ways of checking if the materials you are using are sustainable. The best is "thinking small." By this I mean that often the closer to you the material has grown or been harvested, the more sustainable it is to use, since it hasn't had to be flown, shipped, or driven to you, minimizing pollutants and fuel use.

Recyclability

If the material cannot be renewed easily, can it be recycled? An example of this is metals, since they can be reclaimed and still retain high quality. This means that we put less strain on these resources being harvested and instead use the same material again and again.

Design for Utility

I have based my practice on designing with utility in mind. The reason for this is simple: If we value a tool and it brings us joy to use, not only are we going to be drawn to use that tool each time, but the material gets used to its fullest potential, making it less likely to be discarded or replaced easily. This ensures the material is used for a lifetime or more; in addition, the happiness that comes with regularly using something that you have made yourself brings a satisfaction and independence that everyone deserves to feel.

Designing your versions of the pieces explained in this book, then going on to design more handmade items for your home, requires careful thought. Here are a few questions I like to consider when designing:

How will it be used?

How will this item interact with you? If you are going to hold it, maybe you want to consider whether you prefer the feeling of soft curves or clean lines. I like to design anything that will be held by the user to feel nice in the hand. It should have a good heft to it—not be too light or too heavy—and I like to make different sizes for different preferences.

How will it be placed?

Will it sit on a shelf or hang on a hook? Both of these options require designing—either a flat surface for the item to sit on, or a hanging loop or hole to hang with. I like to ensure there is a way to hold each piece I make, so that it can sit on a shelf to be seen, or hung in the utility room ready for use when needed.

How will you care for it?

Will this item come into contact with food? If so, it's important to think about the finish, the washing, all the pieces that go into making it: Are they water-resistant or can you make them? Some people worry about washing wood, but as long as you know how to wash it—no submerging, no dishwashers, and no harsh chemicals—you're good to go!

What's your aesthetic?

Finally, you want something to look good in your home and bring you joy every time you look at it and use it. Are you a minimalist through and through, wanting to just admire the simplicity of the wood grain? Or are you a colorful soul wanting to add character and color to every room? I like to offer a range of finishes to my designs to ensure there is something for everyone. Natural wood grain brings a subtle warmth and neutrality to any room, while a colorful pop on a piece may add a bit of eccentricity and fun to your design.

Answering these questions alone will give some idea of how the item might look, and give you a starting point for designing pieces in the future. It happens all too often that you buy a beautiful thing to use in your home but, when you get back, discover it's not actually practical to use. I hope that this simple questioning process will allow the items you design and make to fit perfectly in your home, your hand, and your life!

Health and Safety

When working with wood and fibers, there are some important general rules of health and safety to note. The biggest one is PPE—personal protective equipment. This generally means mask, goggles, and ear protection. Because we are working with mainly hand tools, ear protection isn't essential but is always good to have in your tool kit. The mask needs to be fitted to cover your nose and mouth. You will need to wear a mask with an FFP3 filter (N99 US equivalent) when working with hardwoods. You must wear goggles whenever there is a risk of flying debris, but also when there is a risk of flying sawdust making its way into your eyes. Goggles, mask, and ear protection are all essential when woodturning.

When working with anything sharp, you need to be aware at all times of where you are directing the sharp end of the tool. Sharp tools also need to be stored somewhere safe where they cannot fall and injure someone or be bumped by mistake. It's a good idea to have all your tools mounted on the wall, using a pegboard or magnet screws. This reduces the likelihood of you leaning over the bench and catching yourself on something sharp, and also means the blade edges stay protected and out of the way of other tools and materials.

When working on the lathe, keep your work spinning at the right speed to reduce the likelihood of the chisel coming toward you if the work slips. When working with carving chisels, always push away from yourself and never use force to pull the chisel in the direction of your body.

An important note: The images in this book have been taken so you can clearly see the described techniques in use. Before you start any of the practical applications of working with a tool, technique, or project, it is essential that the wood you are working on is secured either by a vise or a clamp for safety purposes. Never skip this step.

Stance is an important part of working with tools—particularly planes, lathes, and saws. A comfortable, dynamic stance helps prevent injury. In order to have a comfortable stance, you need to set your work at the right height. Your feet need to be positioned the width of your shoulders apart, with one foot slightly in front of the other. Not only is it easier to work in this position, but it's safer. If something—a tool or a piece of wood, for example—slips or falls, having one foot in front of the other allows you to step away more easily. If your feet are together when something falls, you have to make more of a lunge to move away, increasing the likelihood of injury.

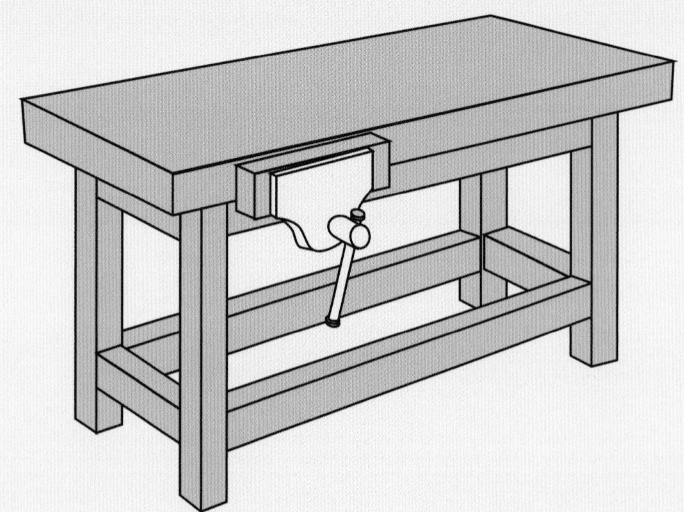

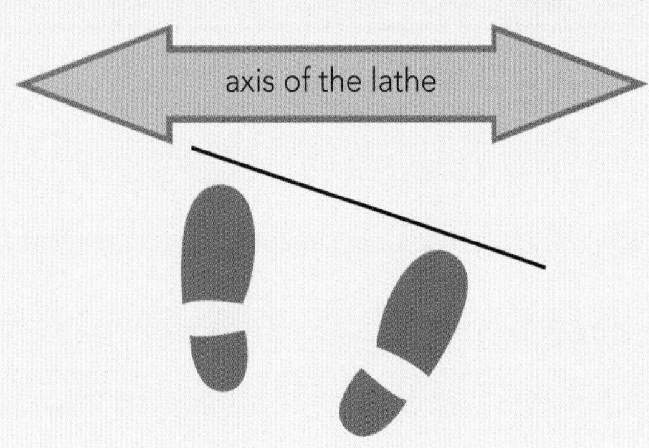

Clamps and Vises

Securing work safely to the work bench gives you full control of the project while working. The best way to do this is by using clamps or a vise. Clamps come in a variety of shapes and sizes, and are a simple (usually threaded) mechanism that holds your work onto a surface such as a workbench.

A G-clamp (also known as a C-clamp) is a versatile and useful clamp (see opposite page) to have in a tool kit. They are usually used at least two at a time to stop work from swivelling on the work bench. G-clamps are essential for securing wood while you saw, file, drill, or sand the work.

Another way of securing work is by using a vise (illustration above). Vises are usually bolted to the workbench. They have a simple threaded mechanism similar to a clamp, but because they're bolted to the bench, you can really push against the work without moving it. I find when planing larger pieces, a vise is really useful. Vises also allow work to be clamped upright, which makes it easier to work on end grain and edge grain.

Finally, attention is the most important part of working with tools. Mistakes happen, but as long as you are attentive to what you are doing, you can move away, turn off the machine, or point the tool away from yourself before getting injured. Paying close attention to the blade or tool also allows for a better finish, since this way you can feel where the tool is and what it is doing.

WOODWORKING 101

This chapter is a brief introduction to a basic tool kit. If you have worked with wood before and have a good understanding of these basics, feel free to jump right into the Project Techniques on page 52. However, if you're starting from scratch, this chapter should help not only identify some of the tools used throughout the book, but also give an idea of wood structure, some basic tools for your tool kit, and some basic techniques.

MADE IN JAPAN
ライフソー HI
両刃250 ハードインパルス
MADE IN JAPAN

Wood Grain

Let's start with wood grain. "Grain" refers to the fibers of the wood, which illustrate the direction of growth of the tree. If you imagine that a tree trunk is actually made of a tightly packed bundle of long, usually straight, fibers, when working with wood, try to picture this to orient how you want to cut it. Cutting along these fibers is called a rip cut (this goes between the lengths of fiber). Cutting across these fibers is a crosscut (this severs the fibers). Every time you cut timber with a crosscut, you will expose "end grain," and every time you cut timber with a rip cut, you will expose "face grain" or "edge grain."

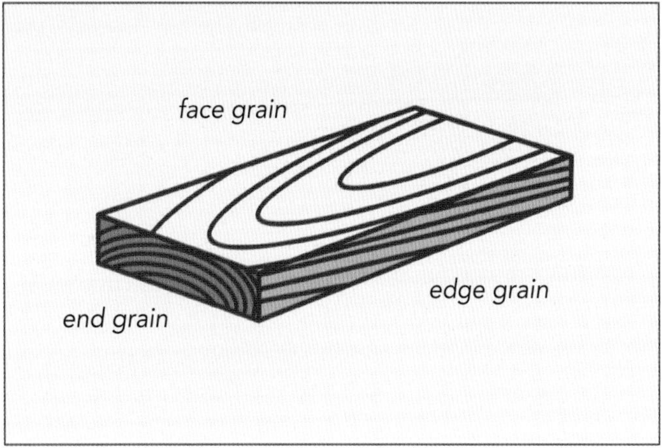

Picture end grain as the end of the tightly packed fibers (similar to a bundle of brushmaking fiber). When you look down on end grain from above, you see a portion of what may be familiar as the growth rings of the tree. Picture face grain (or edge grain) as the length of the trunk being split in two along its full length.

The difference between face and edge grain is how the lengths of fibers are exposed—face grain is the growth rings intercepting the surface and gives the look of irregular patterns in the grain. Edge grain usually runs relatively straight and slightly diagonally, depending on species and grain pattern. "Knots" and "character" in timber have different pros and cons. For the work explained in this book, most knots and character add a nice aesthetic to a piece. However, for future reference, knots create weaker spots in the grain, since it interrupts the stronger straight-grain fibers. They can also be hard to work around and blunt tools. "Tear-out" happens when the fibers of the wood tear rather than cut smoothly. It creates splintering or undulations where you don't want them, and can create a rough surface. Tear-out happens for a variety of reasons: It may be because the wood is cut against the grain instead of with the grain, or it may be due to blunt tools or difficult grain patterns.

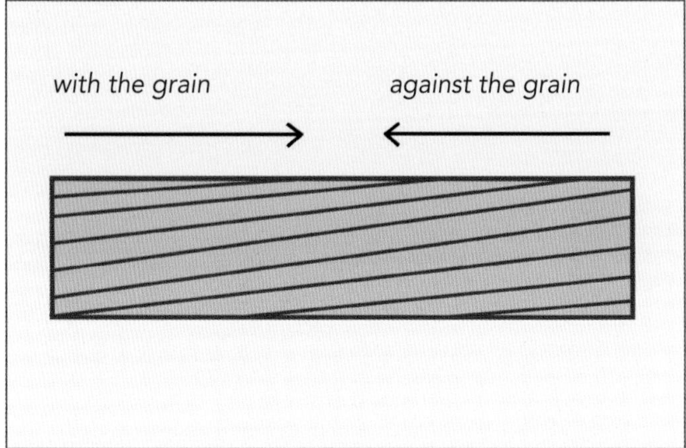

When we explain working "with the grain" or "against the grain," we are talking about the direction of the flow of fibers within the face or edge grain. Think about it like stroking a dog or cat: Pet them in the direction the hairs grow, and it feels smooth, but pet them the other way and it's uncomfortable for you and the animal. When working with the grain, you are working from the "low end" to the "high end" of the grain direction.

The growth rings of a tree, referred to as "end grain" once the log is turned into timber.

Left: When considering which wood to use for a project, it is important to think about the grain structure. Every species of tree has its own unique grain structure and, within that, varying grain depending on the seasonal growth of the tree.

Below: End grain—closest to you—and face grain along the length of the timber.

Wood Types

To begin with, it is helpful to know the difference between softwood and hardwood. Softwood comes from coniferous trees, meaning they have needle-like leaves; examples are pine and fir. Hardwood comes from deciduous trees, which drop their leaves during colder months—for example, oak and ash. Softwood, as its name implies, is softer and tends to have more uniform grain than hardwood. Hardwood is dense and strong and can have a lot of variety and patterning through the grain.

When considering any woodworking project, it is important to know the suitability of the wood for its intended use. Softwoods, although softer than hardwoods, can be extremely strong and versatile and are brilliant for use in construction, flooring, lower-cost furniture, and toys. They are commonly used in instrument making. Hardwoods take longer to grow, so are more expensive and tend to be used for flooring, high-end furniture, boat building, tools, and utensils.

For the projects in this book, I would suggest using mainly hardwood—softwood utensils and chopping boards are not as durable and don't hold up to the same daily use that hardwoods will.

Ash

American or white ash (*Fraxus americana*) is a fast-growing deciduous tree that produces relatively inexpensive, even-textured, straight-grained, light-gray-brown, slightly coarse timber. It is employed when strength is important and is often used for tool handles, flooring, and sports equipment, such as baseball bats. The timber is flexible when steamed and is often used for making furniture, since it glues and stains well. Although strong and durable, it is vulnerable to insect attack and not suitable for outdoor use unless well finished.

Beech

Beech (American = *Fagus grandifolia*; European = *Fagus sylvatica*) is a great hardwood to start with. It has a light reddish tone and a tight grain. This doesn't blunt your tools as quickly as oak will, and it sands and polishes to a smooth finish. Beech is commonly used in furniture and gives a similar aesthetic to oak when oiled in a particular way, so is commonly used as a substitute. Often the wooden spoons, spurtles, and lemon reamers found in decor and interior hardware stores are made from beech wood.

Cherry

American cherry (*Prunus serotina*) is a hardwood cherished for its dark, rich timber, which deepens and improves with age as the heartwood oxidizes. The timber is strong and durable, is not too hard to work, and resists warping and shrinking. For this reason, cherry is often used for furniture and high-quality objects. It is a durable and long-lasting wood with fine, straight, close grain, sometimes appearing in waves and curls. European cherrywood is much paler and tends to yellow tones rather than reds. Cherry wood is more costly than other readily available timbers and requires experience to work well with. Other fruit woods such as applewood are also good options.

Hickory

Although growing from a deciduous tree, hickory (*Carya ovata*) is one of the heaviest, hardest, and strongest woods native to America. It has wide natural variations in brown colors and is hard to work and hard to damage. This makes it ideal for tools, weapons, flooring, and furniture. It is synonymous with baseball bats. Hickory is difficult to work with due to its interlocked and stringy grain, which is prone to warping. In short, it's a timber for the experienced woodworker.

Maple

American hard maple, also often called sugar maple (*Acer saccharum*), is the most commercial of the very many maple species. The timber is hard and dense and a very pale, almost white color, although it can have a golden cast. Its tight, smooth grain is very hard-wearing, which makes it ideal for high-usage natural-flooring areas such as basketball courts, gymnasiums, and public areas like theaters and offices. It is often used for high-end furniture.

Oak

Oak (*Quercus*) is particularly dense and is one of the more commonly known and used hardwoods. It has a slightly open grain with a distinctive pattern and caramel color. It stands up to heavy wear, making it a popular choice in flooring. When you're next in a grand old building with exposed floorboards, take a look at their width. It is common to see up to 20 in. (51 cm)-wide floorboards. This kind of width in oak would not be found now, since the trees available then had been growing for hundreds of years before being cut down. Nowadays, it can be hard to find machined oak wider than 12 in. (30 cm). Because of its slightly open grain, oak isn't best suited to chopping boards or utensils that come in contact with heat, since this can lead to damage. Moreover, oak has a lot of tannins in it, meaning that when it comes into contact with heat, it can start to release these tannins and turn food black. Instead, use oak for its hard-wearing properties and beautiful grain pattern.

Sycamore maple

Acer pseudoplatanus, sycamore maple—simply called "sycamore" in Britain and Europe—provides a smooth and tight-grained wood. It creates a beautiful, silky finish and, because of its tight grain, is strong and versatile as well as being easier to work. Sycamore has a pale-yellow color and a subtle grain. It also often has beautiful character caused by "rippling"—wave patterns that almost look 3D—and "spalting," zone lines and coloration caused by fungi. Sycamore is often used for furniture, veneers, tool handles, and kitchenware. Because of its tight grain, sycamore is great for use in the kitchen as chopping boards and utensils. The tight grain allows very little moisture and bacteria to penetrate the wood and also allows fewer smells to absorb into the grain.

Walnut

Walnut comes in two main types: black and white. Black—*Juglans nigra*, as shown—is a dark wood with distinctive grain patterns that can be irregular. Black walnut is a medium-density timber, distinctively grained with a rich brown color and sometimes wonderful, wavy figuring that takes polish well. It is moderately hard but durable and decay-resistant, although it is susceptible to insect attack. It has many wonderful properties and is immensely popular among woodworkers. When worked, it has a distinctive (although faint) odor and can trigger allergic reactions, most commonly skin irritation and eye problems. It is used for a wide variety of domestic requirements, in particular high-end furniture.

White walnut, commonly known as butternut (*Juglans cinerea*), is a deciduous hardwood tree that's softer than most hardwoods. While not very durable, the white walnut is easy to work with by hand, makes an excellent wood for carving and decorative furniture, and is especially useful for paneling. It is light brown to golden in color, with often-irregular grain that barely shrinks and rarely warps, although it can take stain well.

Fibers and Binding

I recommend using natural plant fibers when planning your brushes and brooms. Aside from being biodegradable and incredibly hard-wearing, plant fibers have amazing qualities that you may not expect. Plant fibers commonly used for brushmaking include the following:

Arenga A firm fiber created from the *Arenga pinnata*, also known as the sugar palm. Incredibly resistant to wear, this fiber has been used for a long time to make ship rope and is also heat resistant up to 150°F (66°C). It is used to reinforce various composites—even concrete—and adds comparative strength to fiberglass. Arenga is a stiffer alternative to tampico and is brilliant for general sweeping around the home, by the hearth, and in the garden. Arenga is grown and processed in Indonesia.

Bassine Comes from the *Borassus flabellifer*, also known as the Palmyra palm. Bassine fiber is one of the stiffest of the plant fibers, with thick, woody strands recognizable from hardware stores' classic garden brooms. Bassine lends itself to heavy-duty scrubbing and sweeping outdoors and over stone or brick floors. Bassine is resistant to water, heat, and chemicals and is produced mostly in southern India.

Broomcorn Botanically known as *Sorghum vulgare*, broomcorn has long been used to create brushes and brooms, so much so that it's become its common name! It grows in tall, increasingly finer stems that are laden with reddish seeds at the tips. These finer ends are dried and seeds are removed to reveal the fine, wavy fibers. Broomcorn is most commonly seen in long-handled sweeping brooms but can also be bound into smaller hand-held brooms. It is brilliant at picking up dirt and debris around the home and garden. Broomcorn is grown in numerous countries around the world.

Arenga (sugar palm)

Bassine (Palmyra palm)

Broomcorn (Sorghum vulgare)

Coco Also known as coir, it comes from the husk of the coconut. Coco fiber is caramel-colored and is somewhere between tampico and arenga in stiffness. This fiber is very water-resistant and rot-resistant, meaning it has a long life and maintains structure even in humid and wet environments. Another advantage of coco is that its source is discarded coconut husks, meaning it is very sustainable to use. Coco is commonly used for natural scourers, since it dries rapidly. It can also be used for sweeping brushes around the home and garden. Coco is grown and processed mainly in Sri Lanka and India.

Tampico This silky fiber is created from the *Agave lechuguilla*, a cousin of the agaves that supply syrup. It has been used for hundreds of years to make cordage, matting, baskets, and more. *Agave lechuguilla* cannot be cultivated, so it is grown naturally and then collected and processed commercially. Tampico is brilliant for wet-cleaning tools such as scrubbing brushes and is naturally antistatic, which means it will collect fine dust from surfaces but will pass on antistatic properties, so the surface will stay cleaner for longer. These brushes are ideal for finer dust, crumbs, and wet cleaning around the home. Tampico is grown in Mexico.

Hemp This is the strongest of the natural fibers. If you want to keep everything completely natural, use hemp cord. Hemp is amazingly strong and resiliant for a natural fiber and was the traditional material used to make canvas for ships' sails. In terms of sustainability, hemp is the way to go, since it grows incredibly quickly and is 100 percent biodegradable. If you are keen to keep everything natural, also look into which dyes are used to color your hemp, since some dyes are not biodegradable. When using hemp, try to find material $^1/_8$ in. (3 mm) in thickness in a twisted cord—this thickness ensures good strength as well as durability for daily use.

Coco (coconut)

Tampico (agave)

Hemp

Nylon This alternative to hemp, although synthetic, holds binding for a lot longer and, when working with tougher fibers, has the strength you may need to bind the fibers securely in place. Nylon has more tensile strength than hemp, meaning it can undergo more pressure for longer without splitting or stretching and losing structural integrity. I use both for different brushes, depending on how solid the binding needs to be and how flexible the fibers are. If you decide to use nylon, work with a $^1/_{16}$–$^1/_8$ in. (2 or 3 mm) twisted cord for best results.

Nylon cord

Drills

When selecting a drill, think about its weight and comfort for holding. If you're looking to build a toolbox full of essentials, a drill is necessary for fundamentals such as drilling pilot holes, making screw holes, and countersinking. If you're keen to keep manual power throughout your projects, choose an eggbeater drill or, if you prefer battery power, go for a cordless hand drill. Drills come with varying settings depending on the make, but the best drills will have torque, speed, and direction settings. Torque will tell the drill how much spinning power to give the bit and is usually shown on a rotating gauge with numbers from 1 to 15, with 1 signifying least torque and 15 signifying most. Speed tells the drill how fast to spin the bit (usually 1 for slow and 2 for fast). Direction tells the drill whether to spin clockwise (forward) or counterclockwise (reverse) and is commonly changed with a sliding toggle near the trigger. When drilling, be aware of the angle of the bit against the wood. Most of the drilling for our projects will be square to the wood. To hone your technique, drill a few tester holes to practice getting a feeling for where square is.

The second part of using a drill effectively is having the right drivers and drill bits. To have a useful toolbox, you need a set of twist drill bits, which can be used on both soft and hardwood, and fit into the chuck jaws at the end of the drill. Twist drill bits usually come in sets, with $^{1}/_{16}$ in. (2 mm) increments going from $^{1}/_{16}$ in. (2 mm) up to around $^{1}/_{2}$ in. (12 mm)-diameter bits. To drill larger holes than this (including the types of holes needed for the chopping board and candle holder projects), consider getting Forster bits, which create a flat-bottomed hole in specific diameters over $^{1}/_{2}$ in. (12 mm).

Driver bits are used to drive fixings into wood and fit into the chuck jaws at the end of the drill. The drivers' ends are made to match the fixing head, the most common being Phillips (X shaped), flat head (- shaped), Torx (* shaped), Pozidriv (variation on X shaped) and Hex (Allen shaped). The best thing to get as a beginner is a set with various heads and sizes. This will set you up not only for woodworking but also for odd jobs around the home.

Files

Important tools to have in your toolbox, files are versatile for shaping and finishing work, and can be used to take rough cuts down to a final form, ready to be sanded. Files come in different shapes and sizes, but all are hardened steel tools with fine rows of teeth. The teeth, when pushed along the wood surface, scrape away fine layers of fiber and help shape the piece quickly and easily. Files are necessary for many of the projects in this book. To start, it's best to buy a set that includes a round file (known as a rat-tail), half-round file, flat file, triangle file, and square file. A simple set like this lets you do all the shaping you should need.

When using a file, the best technique is to hold the handle with your dominant hand and set your non-dominant thumb on the top of the file, pressing down firmly. Apply pressure on the forward stroke and release pressure on the backward stroke. This helps you stay aware of your filing direction and angle, and keeps the file balanced. When working, always be sure to run your file diagonally along the grain direction, since this will remove material without gouging tool marks too deeply into the wood. When you are happy with your shaping, it is time to sand the piece and complete with your choice of finish.

Creating convex curves with a file requires a flat file (or the back of your half-round file); run the file along the cut marks to round the edge into the curve you want.

- Creating a concave curve requires the half-round file or the round file: Run this along the inside of the curve, creating the final shape you want. (1)
- Create square corners by using either a square or flat file. Acute angles are shaped with the triangle file. (2)

1

2

Saws

Saws are a big topic to cover. To narrow it down slightly, we will focus on a few really good handheld saws that are an ideal part of any toolbox. In the Project Techniques section of the book, we look at pull saws or nokogiri, which cut on the pull (traditionally used in Japanese joinery), whereas Western saws cut on the push. In this section I'll give a brief overview of both push and pull versions of each saw and provide some examples of when each is the right one to use.

The biggest difference between push and pull saws is that the former needs more tension in the blade, so the blades are a lot thicker. Pull saws cut under the tension of you pulling back the blade back through the wood, so these blades can be a lot thinner and lighter.

Saws have varying handles, blades, and teeth, which dictate what they are best used for. The handle is usually made from wood, bamboo, or plastic—importantly, this is the only part of the saw you hold when cutting. The blade is the flat metal area, which gives the tool strength or flexibility (or both), depending on the type of saw. The teeth are the sharp edges that protrude from the blade, and these have varying shapes depending on the purpose of the saw.

A hand saw with a Japanese tooth and maple wood planks.

Earlier, when discussing grain (see page 22), I touched on rip cuts and crosscuts. These describe the direction of the cut with reference to the grain direction. This is important information to understand when picking out the right saw for your intended project. A saw made for rip cuts—a rip saw—has large, straight teeth that are made for ripping through the grain (with the grain direction). Rip saws usually have no spine on the back, since you need your blade to pass through the whole length of the wood. You should also notice that on a rip saw there are fewer TPI (teeth per inch), enabling rough and fast cutting. To add this to your toolbox, look for a (hand) rip saw that cuts on the push, or a kataba rip saw (or the finer-bladed tatebiki) for a saw that cuts on the pull.

A saw designed to cut across the grain is known as a crosscut saw. These saws have alternating teeth of varying sizes that are made to create smoother finishes, as well as more TPI, which makes for cleaner cutting. To add this to your toolbox, look for a classic crosscut saw, which cuts on the push, or a kataba crosscut saw (or a thinner plate yokobiki), which cuts on the pull.

Another option is a ryoba saw, which has a double-sided blade: one side created for rip cuts and the other side created for crosscuts. This versatile setup means that you need only one saw in your toolbox.

A final saw to consider is a backsaw. This essentially means that the top edge of the blade is reinforced with a spine, allowing the blade to be thinner, and therefore enabling more precise and accurate cuts. The teeth on a backsaw are also finer, which adds to their ability to cut precisely. The only downside of the spine in the saw is that the blade cannot pass freely through the timber, which means this is limited to doing smaller, more precise, finishing cuts. To add this to your toolbox, look for a tenon saw or dovetail saw for a blade that cuts on the push, or a dozuki saw for a blade that cuts on the pull. (In Japanese, dozuki means "attached trunk"—having a backsaw reinforcement.)

Tenon backsaw with reinforced spine (cuts on the push)

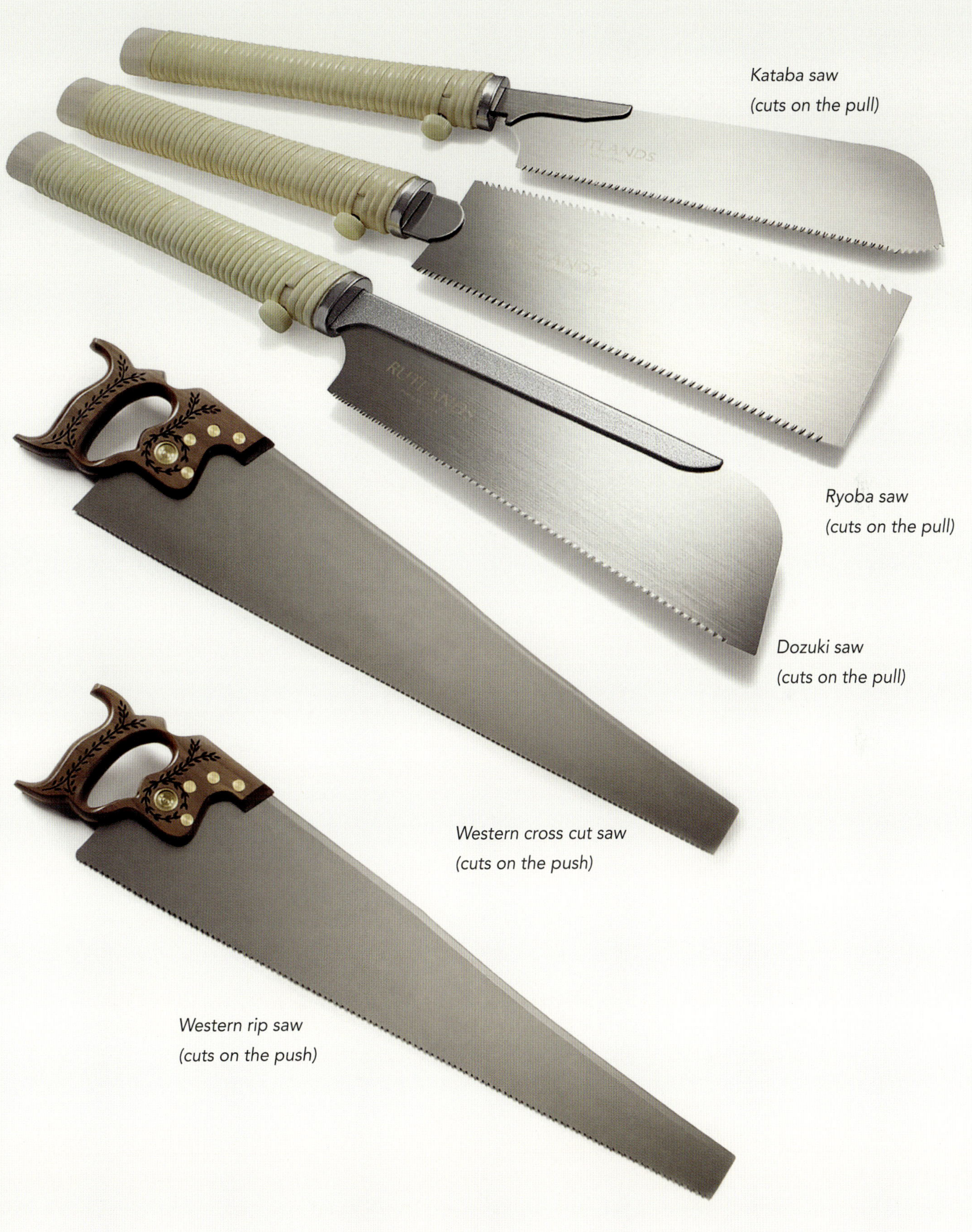
Kataba saw
(cuts on the pull)
Ryoba saw
(cuts on the pull)
Dozuki saw
(cuts on the pull)
Western cross cut saw
(cuts on the push)
Western rip saw
(cuts on the push)

Sanding

Sanding is the process you move on to once you are happy with the shape and final form of the design. It is an easy mistake to think that sanding can be used to change the shape of your item, but this actually takes lots of time and effort for minimal reward. Best practice is to ensure the form is exactly how you want it and is already filed to an even surface before sanding begins. Sanding is done to transform the surface of the wood into something smooth and polished.

Before even starting sanding, an important thing to consider is the direction to sand in. When needing to remove a lot of material, sand at a 45-degree angle to the direction of grain. However, bear in mind that this will leave deeper scratches that will need more sanding to remove afterward. For removing smaller amounts of material—and as you get to higher grits—work along the direction of grain. When sanding end grain (especially when using a sanding block), work inward to ensure you don't get tear-out at the edges of the workpiece.

Sandpaper is categorized and graded by number and begins at lower 40-60 (coarse), through 80-120 (medium), 120-150 (fine), 150-220 (very fine), 280-320 (extra fine), all the way up to 600. The lower the number, the larger the abrasive particles on the sandpaper, meaning the more material they will remove, and the rougher surface it will create. The higher the number, the smaller the abrasive particles on the sandpaper, meaning they will remove less material and will instead polish out the surface to create a silky-smooth finish.

When woodworkers talk about "working up the grits," it is a quick way of saying that we intend to sand our piece starting with a low grit and work all the way up to a high grit, utilizing all the grits in between. Another common mistake is sanding with an 80 and then moving straight into a 320 and expecting it to polish out your 80-grit scratches; this will not work, since a 320-grit is not coarse enough to polish 80-grit scratches. This is why we work our way gradually up the grits, using each grit in between, since a 120 has the capacity to polish out 80 scratches, a 180 has the capacity to polish out 120 scratches, etc. This leaves you with a fully polished surface with no scratches left from previous work.

Using a sanding block is a helpful and simple way of keeping edges sharp when sanding. This is especially helpful when sanding something that needs to stay flat, and you don't want to round out any precise corners. There are blocks specifically for this purpose, which have a small lip to allow you to wrap the sandpaper around the block. Otherwise, simply get a small, flat piece of wood and wrap the sandpaper around it, ensuring it overlaps so you can hold the edges in place.

60
60
60
100
150
150
220
180
200
400
100
400

Finishing

Finishing work is always something that takes an unexpectedly long time, but it is a valuable step that refines and gives a curated look. Finishing can be done in a number of ways, with the most usual process being oil and wax. I like to use tung oil on all my work, since this hardens deep into the grain and ensures a long and hard-wearing finish. Waxing can be done after oiling and provides an even more hard-wearing and water-resistant finish to your work.

Foodsafe Oils

Tung oil This is a natural drying oil pressed from the seeds of the tung tree (*Vernicia fordii*), which is native to China. It has been used for centuries in Asia as a wood finish and waterproofing oil. When exposed to oxygen, tung oil polymerizes (hardens), forming a durable, water-resistant surface.

Mineral oil A clear, odorless, non-drying oil made from petroleum distillates. It is sold as food-grade (in other words, safe for food preparation) mineral oil. Unlike tung or linseed oil, mineral oil does not cure or harden; it always stays liquid inside the wood and must be periodically reapplied.

Raw linseed oil This is the natural oil pressed from flax seeds (the same plant that gives us linen and flax fiber, *Linum usitatissimum*). It's a drying oil, meaning it reacts with oxygen to polymerize and harden inside the wood. It's one of the oldest wood finishes used worldwide.

Non-Food-Safe Oils for Furniture

Danish oil This oil is a blend of a hardening oil, similar to linseed, plus varnish and solvents. This allows the oil to penetrate and leave a shiny finish on the surface of the wood. It is not safe to use for things that will come into contact with food.

Teak oil As with Danish oil, this is a blend of a hardening oil and solvents that allow it to penetrate deeper into wood fibers. It is usually used on dense woods like teak or mahogany, and is great for outside use on decking or doors.

Boiled linseed oil Not to be confused with raw linseed oil. Boiled linseed oil is raw linseed oil mixed with chemical drying agents and is not safe for use around food. Can be used on other furniture around the home.

Wax

Beeswax This is a brilliant wax that can be used on anything around the home, whether it will come into contact with food or not. A favorite method of mine is to melt it slowly in a bain-marie and then add a food-safe oil. This creates a wax blend that will harden, but can be polished into the wood surface more easily than a solid wax. It also gives a lovely, sweet smell to your pieces.

Carnauba wax If you are vegan or don't like to use products from bees, this is a great alternative. It comes from the leaves of the carnauba palm (*Copernicia prunifera*) and hardens to form a shiny, protective layer over the wood. It is food-safe and can be blended with oils to create a natural, safe finish.

Candelilla wax Another plant-based wax that is neither as soft as beeswax nor as hard as carnauba wax. It comes from the candelilla shrub (*Euphorbia antisyphilitica*) and has been used to create lip balms, lipsticks, and other beauty products. It is food-safe and can be blended with oils to create a natural, safe finish.

Finishing work can also come in the form of adding color. Milk paint is a natural, food-safe paint that has been used for thousands of years, from cave paintings to artifacts in King Tutankhamen's tomb. It is a blend of milk protein (casein) and natural pigments, along with other natural additions to the recipe. Milk paint comes in standard powdered colors, to which you simply add water to create a good consistency for painting. It is very quick to dry, which can be convenient but frustrating if you mix too much—so mix only a small amount each time you use it. Pigments are available in varying colors, but there's nothing to stop you from blending your own. Depending on your color theory confidence, you can mix your own to color-match something you have in your home already. For example, try coordinating your new utensils to your kitchen cabinet color. Once you have painted two coats of milk paint, leave it to dry between coats, then apply a thin layer of oil of your choice and let this soak in. It's ready.

A final finishing alternative comes in the form of yakisugi. This is a Japanese technique meaning "burnt cedar" and allows the woodworker to seal their project by charring the surface. See pages 94–99 for more background on this technique and how to successfully use it without accidentally turning your work into ash!

PROJECT TECHNIQUES

This is an introduction to the core tools and techniques featured in the rest of the book. There are ideas for projects that will familiarize you with using these tools and give the opportunity to experiment with the processes involved. I will provide clear ideas for using a range of basic tools that will build a strong foundation for all manner of projects.

It is easy to go to a hardware store and get yourself some tools to build a kit, but once back home, when you need to use them on a specific project, it can feel daunting. Even the depths of the internet can't always give you the answer to the exact question you have, or troubleshoot a particular issue. This is why passing on knowledge in a physical or visual way is imperative to ensure these crafts and skills continue. I was taught what I know in woodworking and brushmaking not by any schooling or exams, but by being alongside someone who was willing to teach me. I hope these pages will act as your guide to refining your skills through a selection of versatile tools and techniques.

As noted in the health-and-safety section, please remember that the images in this book have been taken so you can see the technique being used and described. Sometimes this meant removing clamps to give a clear view. It is essential that before you start working with a tool or new technique, or starting a project, the wood is secured either by a vise or a clamp for safety purposes. Never skip this step.

Step Structure and Fiber Length

Binding plant fibers together with twine or cord to create a brush or broom is an ancient craft still seen in many cultures around the world. We still have artifacts displayed in museums intact from the second century BCE, showing palm fiber bound with plant cord. In many traditions, including Shintoism, feng shui, and Hinduism, the act of sweeping with a broom or brush represents removing old and negative energies to make way for positive and divine energy. Moreover, we should not forget the Celtic and pagan traditions which hold brooms as sacred tools that hold magical properties. The history of these tools is fascinating, and in all parts of the world, as a universal society, we seem to have picked up on the significance of the broom.

In the brush-binding chapter, you will learn how to create a stepped hand broom. These steps create a fan of bristles, which in turn creates a great sweeping motion in the broom. In this section, I provide suggestions for how to change the step structure and length of fiber to create brooms for different uses around the home.

Idea 1. The first variable is the number of steps in a brush. This alters the fan as well as the firmness of the brush. Consider creating a bound brush using three, two, or just one step, and see how the brush becomes narrower as the steps reduce. Also experiment with the size of the steps: Fewer and heavier steps create a narrow but firmer bristle. Shown on the right is a binding over coco fiber, with one step that creates a narrow brush.

Idea 1

Idea 2. The next variable to think about is where the binding starts on the broom. In the first brush project on page 104, the broomcorn starts halfway down; instead, consider binding right at the bottom of the fiber, creating more of a stiff scrubbing or pot brush. By the way, coco is a great fiber for making a scourer or pot brush. Shown are three small scrubbing brushes made with arenga fibers, each with two steps and binding beginning at the base to create a very stiff scrubbing brush.

Idea 2

Idea 3. Think about how you are going to use the brush and whether it would benefit from a mixture of fibers. Fibers can be mixed together to create a gradient of bristle that lends itself to multiple uses around the home. For example, when looking to create a stiff garden brush that also picks up fine soil and debris, consider using bassine with a mixture of arenga. Pictured is a mixture of arenga and tampico combined to create a striped center-stepped brush.

Idea 4. Consider moving the steps to create different patterns within the broom for a striking aesthetic effect. In the first project (page 104), we added each step on the side of the last bound step; however, you can alternate the side of the broom that you add on to create a pyramid effect in the broom. To do this, just add each step to the penultimate step you bound in. This is also illustrated in the brush here.

Ideas 3 and 4

Idea 5. Think aboout the binding material. We experiment later in the book with wire-drawn settings in a wooden handle, but you can also utilize wire to bind brushes. To do this, you need pliers to keep the wire taut, but other than this, you can use all the same techniques as with cord-bound brushes. Shown on the right is a copper-wire-bound brush made from arenga fiber. I constantly use this as my workbench brush in the workshop.

Idea 5

Pull Saws

Pull saws—nokogiri in Japanese—are traditional Japanese woodworking tools. Unlike saws commonly used in the West, pull saws cut on the pull rather than the push. This means the blade cuts under a lot of tension, and so can utilize a more delicate and flexible blade. There are multiple advantages to this, including being able to use the flexibility to butt up to a joint more easily and make a precise cut. It is physically easier to use, since it is more natural to pull under tension rather than push. These saws also have more delicate teeth, so they leave a smoother and better-finished cut.

The best general pull saw is a double-bladed saw, also known as a ryoba (illustrated right), which has a crosscut blade on one edge and a rip-cut blade on the other. There are multiple versions of the ryoba, but nearly all have replaceable blades. Another bonus to the ryoba saw is that there is no spine on the blade, so it can be used to cut through all thicknesses of wood. They are a fantastic tool to have in any woodworking kit, as well as being light and portable.

Notice that on a ryoba saw, there are two blades that have slightly different tooth layouts. One side of the blade has larger, straight, aligned teeth—for rip cuts, or with-the-grain cuts. The other side of the blade has smaller, alternating teeth—this is for crosscuts or across-the-grain cuts.
Before using a ryoba, practice on a spare piece of wood to get comfortable with the tool and familiar with its qualities before choosing your project timber.

ライフソー
両刃250
MADE IN JAPAN

1. Your work bench must be at a comfortable height for you to work at: What is good for a tall person will not be safe or comfortable for a short person. Make any necessary adjustments to ensure your shoulder isn't hunched or working at an uncomfortable angle. The first thing to think about before using any hand tool or machinery is stance. Body position makes all the difference to safety when operating potentially dangerous equipment. For example, a pull saw needs a relaxed stance with one foot in front of the other to keep evenly balanced, and your dominant shoulder needs to be hanging at a natural height.

2. Find a piece of wood to practice cutting. Start with something flat and square, since this is the best starting point for pull-saw practice. With the work clamped at a comfortable height, mark out the first cut. Use a sharp pencil and a steel rule, set square, or angle finder set to 90 degrees. Mark the wood where you need to cut on the two axes that face you. These marks need to be square and aligned to each other.

3. Pick up the saw in your dominant hand and select the appropriate side of the blade to make the cut you need. Resting your non-dominant thumb upright on the wood, butt your blade up to your thumb. I like to use my thumbnail or knuckle to ensure the softer pad of my thumb doesn't get caught on the blade. Your thumb acts as a guide to stabilize the first few cuts. Do not skip this step.

1

2

3

4. The first few cuts will make a groove in the wood for the rest of the blade to follow, so it's essential to get these cuts correct. With the first cut, push the saw away from you to make a groove: The blade is less likely to jump than if you pull down to immediately cut. Do this a couple of times to create a straight and neat groove. Once you have a small groove for the blade to cut into, move your thumb guide away and start to pull and push the blade through the wood. A good tip for keeping the blade straight is to keep an eye on the reflection of the wood in your blade; if the reflection creates a straight line, you know you are cutting straight.

5. As you continue cutting, keep an eye on the movement of the blade. If it feels comfortable, use both hands on the handle to make the cut. Ensure you are square to the piece of wood, and your shoulders are the only thing moving—no rotating or pushing down; the blade does this for you. Try to erase the line you made earlier.

6. Near the end of the cut, slow the saw movement so as not to rip through the bottom of the wood. Practice makes perfect with these saws. If you are used to a saw that cuts on the push, it can seem counterintuitive to relax on the push, but give it time and muscle memory will kick in and you will get square, easy cuts in no time.

7. The finished piece.

4

5

6

7

coasters

An easy starting point, coasters are an essential part of everyday life—for everything from hot coffee cups or teapots to wine or other drinking glasses. Since coasters don't often need washing or come into contact with food, you can select a more characterful piece that will be more of a statement on the table. Things like knots and rippling—even cracks—can look great as a statement on something simple like a coaster, as long as it is stable. Character's one thing, but red wine on a carpet thanks to a wonky coaster doesn't bear thinking about!

Materials:

Clamps, file, pencil, sandpaper, saw, set square, wood; finishing material of your choice

Creating a Coaster

1. Flat, level shapes of wood are needed to make coasters: Anything uneven means trouble for a mug or glass. To ensure this, start with wood that has been machined to the correct thickness. If you are collecting from an offcuts pile, look for something that is around a half-inch (13mm) thickness.

2. Mark out the shape on the chosen wood. Think about something that suits your decor, but also about how large the surface needs to be to support your mugs and glasses—go no smaller than 3 inches (76mm) across. Also, think about how many coasters you want to make in your set. I made a set of four.

3. Once your design is chosen and drawn, begin to use the technique described on pages 60–61 to cut out your design, cutting as close to your line as possible.

4. If the design has straight lines, finish these with a file. Use sandpaper to work up through the grits until you are pleased with the finished surface.

   Choose your final finish and apply. This could be milk paint, yakisugi, or just natural oil.

1

2

3

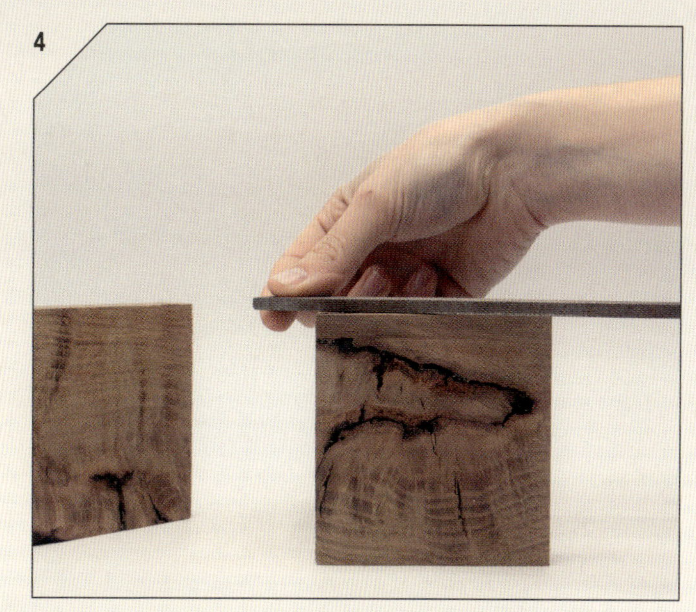

4

Hand Planes

Coming in all shapes and sizes, hand planes are a very versatile tool. They are predominantly used for shaping or smoothing wood, and versions of the planes we use now have been around for thousands of years. Block planes with low angles are particularly useful. These are a small, simple shape that can fit easily into any toolbox and tend to be a comfortable grip for one- or two-handed work. They are made mainly for finer finishing: squaring up edges and chamfering, which is what we will practice in this section. They are also brilliant for finishing proud joints or dowels.

The illustration below shows a block plane and the location of its main visible elements. This is the terminology used in the projects:

Body: The main body of the plane
Heel: The back of the plane, which faces you during use.
Mouth: The opening in the sole of the plane where the blade protrudes
Sole: The bottom, flat face of the plane, which comes into contact with the wood
Throat: Just above the mouth, where shavings exit
Toe: The front of the plane, which makes first contact with the wood

Block planes allow you to adjust the blade depth with the depth-adjusting nut located at the heel of the plane. This will determine how fine your cuts are by adjusting how far the blade protrudes from the mouth of the plane. When starting out, make sure the blade does not protrude too far, since this allows you to get used to how the plane works before you start to remove substantial amounts of material. At the throat of the plane, there are two set screws that allow you to adjust the angle of the blade to ensure a square cut. You also use these to remove the blade for sharpening.

Be aware of the wood grain when using a plane. Where possible, you want to plane your wood with the grain, since cutting against the grain will cause tear-out—when the wood isn't shaved but torn out in chunks. Some characterful grains can create challenges, but there is usually a way around the problem. End grain can also pose difficulties. The main thing to remember is to work inward, from the edge of the piece toward the center from all sides. This ensures that the grain does not split and tear out when you get to the edges.

When using a plane, it is good to get used to a regular hand placement, since this makes it easier to "feel" the wood under the plane. I find that the best and most comfortable hand position is with my dominant hand cupping the heel of the plane and my non-dominant thumb resting at the toe of the plane, giving balanced pressure. Use natural beeswax on the sole of your plane to ensure that the tool glides easily across the wood.

In this section, we will get comfortable with a hand plane and then get creative to style a table centerpiece for candles or flowers.

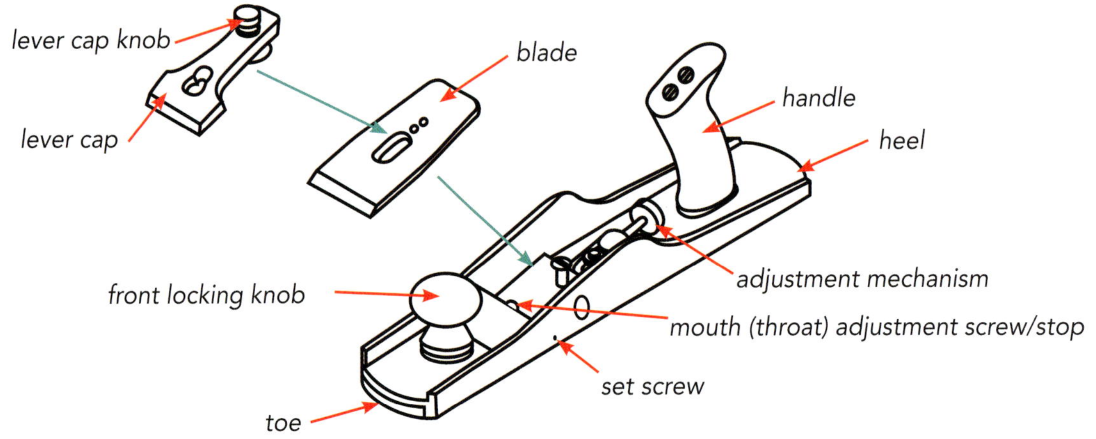

James
QUICKGRIP

1. As mentioned on page 18, stance is the key element to getting your technique right. As when using a pull saw, place one foot in front of the other, with a balanced and neutral stance, ensuring your work piece is at the right height for your arms to have a slight bend in them when working. Get a scrap piece of square hardwood and clamp it down using hand clamps or a vise, so that you are working along the wood grain to start, not on end grain.

2. Back your blade all the way off, using the depth adjustment nut and visually checking down the length of the sole. Never run your hand down the length of the sole from toe to heel to check where the blade is. You can either check visually, using one eye to look down the sole of the plane, or run your thumb carefully from heel to toe.

3. Hold the plane with your dominant hand cupping the heel and your non-dominant thumb giving pressure on the toe. Start with the plane toe on the corner of the wood. First, practice creating a chamfer. To do this, hold the plane at a 45-degree angle and run along the grain, ensuring the blade is not in contact yet. Run your blade down the wood and, between each run, tighten the depth adjustment nut slightly until you start to feel that the blade is coming into contact with the wood.

   Keep the blade at a shallow depth and run the plane down the wood: Stay aware of the pressure you are putting on the wood. You want to ensure that when you start your run, you keep pressure at the toe of the plane, and at the end of the run, you keep pressure at the heel of the plane. This will create a straight and neat chamfer. If you were to do this in reverse and had pressure at the heel on entry and at the toe on exit, you would begin to plane a curve into the wood. When creating a chamfer, count the number of passes, since this will allow you to re-create the same-sized chamfer on every side.

1

2

3

4. Turning your piece, begin to work on the end grain. End grain is harder to plane and can feel resistant. This may be a good time to update the wax on the bottom of your plane, so the sole glides more easily. Start at the edge of the piece and work into the middle on the end grain face. Then move to working on the chamfer, using the same technique and repeating the same amount of passes you used before.

5. Work around the piece, smoothing and chamfering until you are happy with the final result.

4

candle holder

Tactile and practical, wood lends itself perfectly to holding candles, incense sticks, or decorations. With its statement angles and clean lines, this candle holder is a good way to practice planing techniques. Choose a wood with an interesting grain. Make sure it's weighty enough that it won't fall over easily once the candles are in place.

Materials:

Bradawl, clamps, drill with suitable drill bit, file, hand plane, pencil, ruler, sandpaper, wood; finishing material of your choice

1

2

Candle Holder

1. When you feel comfortable and confident with your planing technique, find a nice piece of hardwood for your candle holder. I used a lovely little offcut of walnut.

2. Mark out three points close to each corner of the piece. The challenge is to create a completely smooth angle working between these points. This is a great exercise to practice smooth cutting and applying pressure at different points of the plane.

3. Cut the statement angles with the plane.

4. When the statement angles have been cut, mark out the centers of the candle locations for drilling. The hole size needs to accommodate the candle diameter you're going to use. I used a $^{7}/_{8}$ in. (22 mm) drill bit for this, since most tall candles have a diameter of this size. If you use bigger candles, drill a bigger hole.

3

4

5. Drill the holes by lining the center of the drill bit with your marked center.

6. Clean up any edges with some fine-grit sandpaper, being careful not to round out any of your lovely straight-planed cuts. Finish with milk paint, yakisugi, or simply with oil to seal the wood. On my candle holder, I used an abstract milk paint finish.

7. Oil the piece after using yakisugi or milk paint to keep the wood protected; see below.

5

6

Turning

As its name suggests, turning is a method of shaping wood with a lathe, a machine that holds a piece of wood and turns it, allowing the operator to cut away wood more evenly and swiftly than by hand chiseling.

Lathes are amazing tools to work wood on. Using a lathe is not only a fun skill to learn (using the appropriate gear), but it creates a form with minimal cuts. Turning is a quick technique to see your work take shape. The lathes we see now are mostly electric-powered, but before the Industrial Revolution, people used foot-powered pole lathes. Pole lathes have historically played an important part in the manufacture of utensils for cooking and eating, as well as other tools. A street named Coppergate in my home town of York was discovered to be a Viking craft center with jewelers, metalworkers, and, most interestingly, woodworkers and turners. They gave the street its name: Coppergate literally means "street of the cup makers." Moreover, lathes are also used by metalworkers to spin metal, creating a vast range of functional and essential items.

Lathes are also an accessible woodworking tool to have in your workshop. They come in all shapes and sizes, so if you're short on space, you can get a smaller workbench lathe. Alternatively, you can go for a larger one with larger clearance, which will let you make larger pieces such as plates and big bowls.

I am going to take you through the basic components you need to consider if you are moving into lathe work, and how these things will allow you to create the widest variety of functional pieces for your home.

A lathe is a combination of a motor, gears, a bed, a headstock, a tool rest, and a tailstock. The bed is the long cast-iron or steel rails running horizontally. The headstock sits on the left of the bed and holds your spindle, which is turned by the motor to rotate your work. The motor and gears are housed in the headstock, and you will have either manual gears that require you to move the belt, or electronic gears, which have an adjustment knob to change speed. The tail stock sits at the right-hand end of the bed and can be moved up and down the bed to fit the wood's size. The tailstock also has travel in it and, once clamped in place, can be used to give extra pressure. Your tool rest clamps to your bed and has a movable base and head to angle and move up and down the bed, depending on your project's requirements.

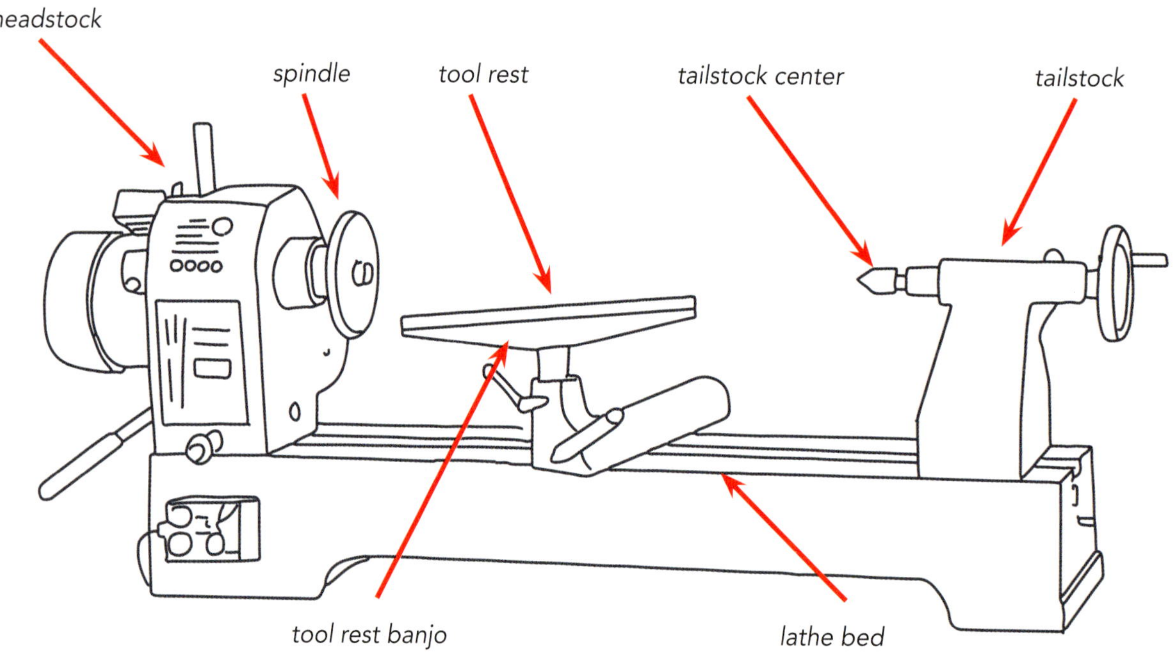

Lathe Components

Having looked at the main elements of the lathe itself, there are a number of smaller components that require a more detailed knowledge. These help hold the wood in the best position for working comfortably and safely. Once in place on the lathe, the wood can then be worked with various types and sizes of chisels.

1. **Chuck jaws** These screw onto the spindle in the headstock and allow you to attach pieces to your lathe. The standard chuck jaw has four dovetail jaws that open and close to hold the wood in a recess or a spigot. Chuck jaws allow you to securely clamp pieces to your lathe without creating any marks or drill holes in the wood. This is particularly useful in bowl making. Once you have turned a spigot or recess in the bottom of the bowl, using the faceplate, you can flip the piece, clamping the spigot or recess to the chuck jaws, and then hollow out and shape the top and inside of the bowl. Chuck jaws also allow you to hold on to dowel-shaped pieces so you can make spindles, handles, small vases, and narrow pieces.

2. **Prong drive center** This pushes into the headstock and gives you either a threaded center to thread into the wood, or a pin center to be clamped into the wood with the help of the tailstock center. Prong drive centers are a functional tool allowing you to clamp your piece between this and your tailstock center, meaning you can work the full length of wood without needing to leave a foot for "parting off." This can be an advantage, especially if the end faces will not be seen. It can also be useful for starting off your turning projects. The first step I take with much of my turning is to use my prong drive center and my tailstock center to rough down the wood and cut a spigot in the base end, to then change over and put the spigot end into the chuck jaws for a secure and centered fit.

3. **Tailstock center** A cone-shaped pin that sits in the tailstock, it gives support when needed to the wood attached to the headstock. Tailstock centers never

1

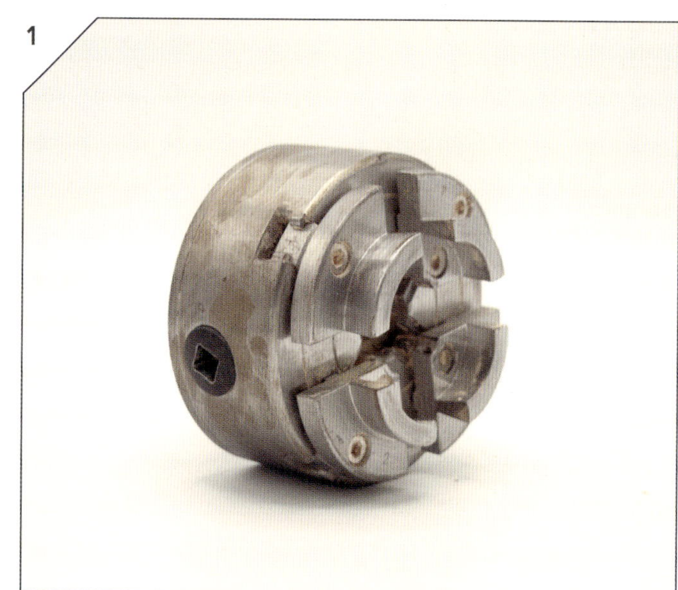

2

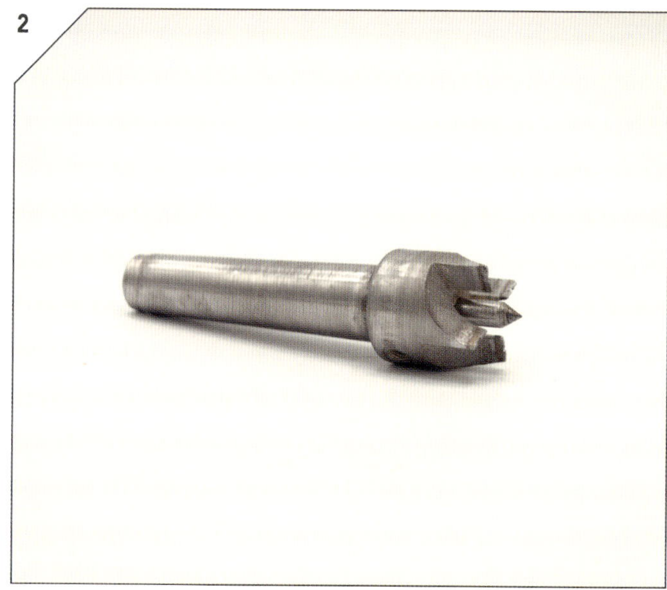

3

hold the wood, but instead give support to the piece. This might be through clamping it to the prong drive center, or centering the end after attaching the piece back onto the chuck jaws. The only time I don't use a tailstock center to help give support is when I am face turning (turning over the lathe bed); for example, when hollowing out a bowl or plate, or shaping the top of a vase. A tailstock center keeps your piece sitting square and straight and is useful when starting off turning projects before you have created a spigot or recess to move to the chuck jaws.

4. **Tailstock drill chuck** It looks like the end of a pillar drill, but with an insert on the opposite end to attach it to the tailstock. The drill chuck holds a drill bit in its jaws and is attached to the tailstock, which can then be used to wind into the top end of a piece and create a centralized hole. It is useful for anything you may be making that needs a central hole drilling. Examples might be a candle holder, vases, smaller containers, or ring boxes.

5. **Faceplate** This screws onto the spindle in the headstock and has a round, flat plate with three or four mounting holes. You can screw the faceplate onto a blank, screw the faceplate to the headstock and have no need for a tailstock center. This is ideal for starting the process of turning a bowl, since you can attach the blank to the faceplate and turn the bottom of the bowl on the open end, turning a spigot or a recess. You then detach the faceplate and attach the chuck jaws to the spindle, clamp the spigot or recess in the chuck jaws, and move to hollowing out the inside and shaping the top lip of the bowl. This is also the process for plates, cups, mugs, and almost anything that you want to hollow out. It removes the screw holes in the hollowing out and finishes the piece with no divots or screw points.

4

5

Using the Lathe

Finding center This needs to be done on the wood, and then again while attaching to the lathe. If working from a square blank and turning something like a vase or spindle, you want to be looking at the end grain and draw two lines joining the opposing corners. Where these lines meet is your center. Do this on both ends and use a center punch to give yourself a small divot at the central points. When attaching the wood to your lathe, use these two central points to align the prong drive center and the tailstock center. When making a bowl or plate, you find the center on the "bottom" and "hollow" sides of the wood.

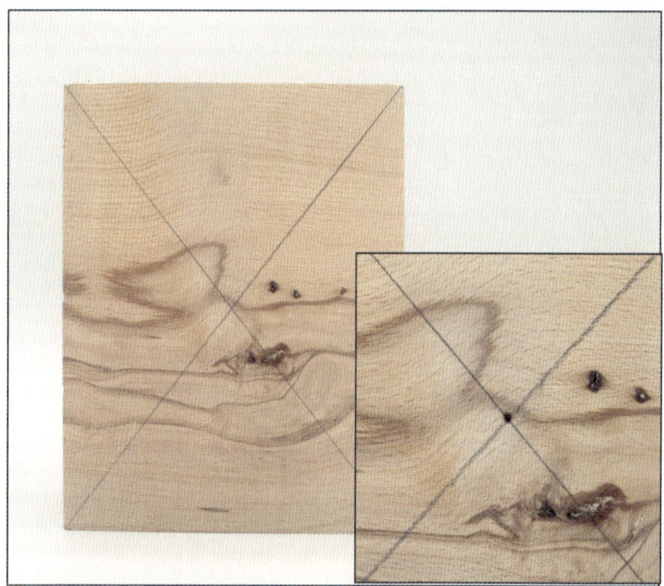

Hand and tool rest placement The tool rest should be set to the middle of the piece's height when attached to the lathe, or just slightly below. The chisels should make contact with the wood at around the middle point, so larger chisels need the tool rest slightly lower. Your hand placement is based on comfort level; your dominant hand is used to hold the chisel down onto the tool rest with the palm facing either down or up, whichever is comfiest. Your nondominant hand, at the base of the handle, guides the chisel left, right, up, and down, and gives pressure when needed for deeper cuts. I am left-handed and use my left hand forward for turning. When face turning, it is easier to be left handed-forward, since this means you can reach over the lathe more easily.

Speeds and gears Speed on the lathe can make all the difference between tear-out and a highly polished, smooth finish. Speed is an important part of turning but is easily overlooked. When starting a piece or roughing out, make sure the speed is low. This ensures minimal vibration on the wood. In turn, this means the wood can come into contact with the chisel easily and create a smoother cut. As the work becomes more refined to the smooth shape you are looking for, you can increase the speed slightly.

The speed should always be calculated depending on the size of the piece you are turning: Use the following equation to figure this out. (D = diameter of piece.)
9000 / D (in inches) = maximum RPMs

Bear in mind, wood with knotted or difficult grain needs slower speeds.Try to avoid putting large pieces on high speeds, since this increases the risk of something flying off the lathe toward you rather than dropping down to the floor.

Chisels

When purchasing a set of chisels, new or secondhand, it is likely that you will have in the set a combination of a roughing gouge, bowl gouges, spindle gouges, a skew, and a parting tool. These combinations allow you to do all the cuts needed to create a wide variety of items.

When beginning a project, start with the large roughing gouge to take off square corners and larger amounts of material. Once completed, move on to the bowl gouges and spindle gouges to create smaller curves or hollowing for bowls or cups. The skew is used for planing a piece and creating a smooth, flat surface. The parting tool is for parting the workpiece from the lathe. It creates a flat cut and is made to cut all the way through the wood.

Cutting action When turning, the chisel you use dictates the angle at which you cut, the height of the tool rest, and the motion of cutting. Using a skew to plane, for example, means finding the cutting angle and moving down the wood without rotating or changing angle. In comparison, when using a bowl gouge or a spindle gouge, the flute always faces the direction of travel along the wood.

Roughing gouge

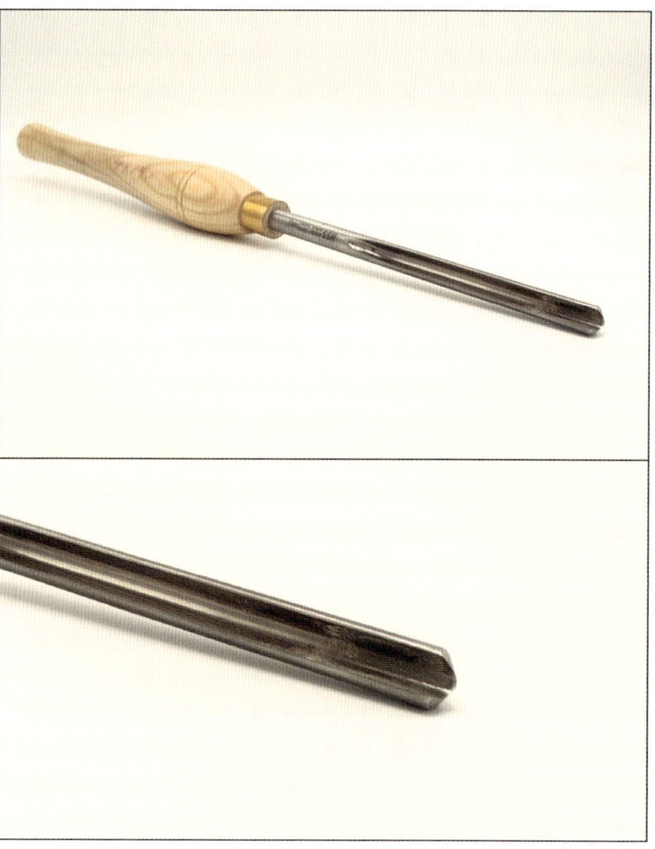

Bowl gouge

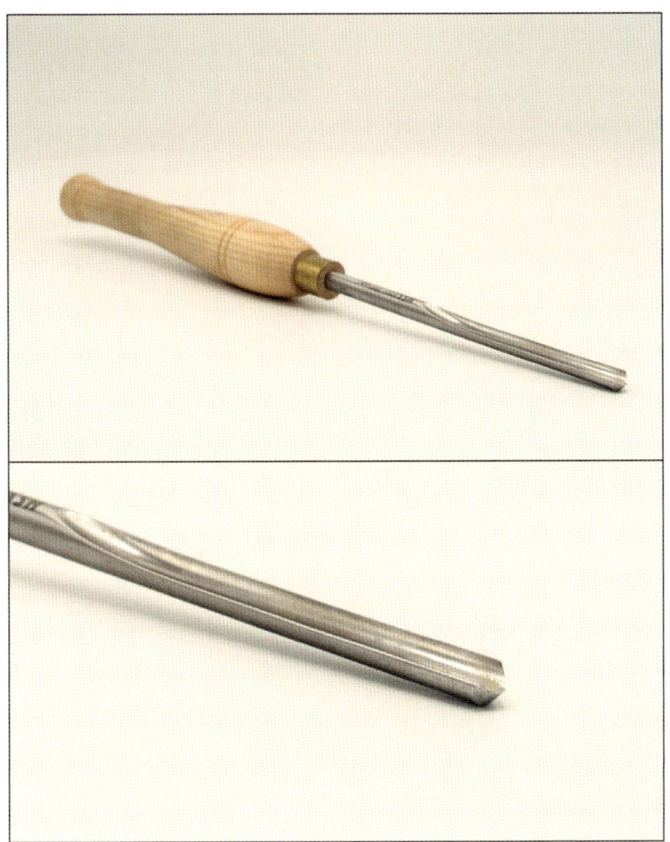

Spindle gouge

Parting tool

Skew

bowl

Wooden bowls make gorgeous, practical gifts. They look complex to make, but once you master the techniques required to use a lathe, they are relatively straightforward. Bowl blanks can usually be found at hardwood timber yards as well as online. And if you are keen to make a bowl in a specific wood, blanks are a good way to avoid having to buy a lot of timber and machine it down yourself.

Materials:

Chisels, lathe and chucks, sandpaper, wood blanks; finishing material of your choice

Creating a Bowl

1. I tend to use offcuts to create my bowls, and you will always find some good offcuts if you are happy to approach a joiner and see what they may have in their burn pile.

   Begin by finding the center of your blank on the side that will eventually be the hollow of the bowl.

2. Screw the faceplate to the chosen hollow side, ensuring it is central to the blank.

3. Attach the faceplate to the spindle. Bring the tool rest to the correct (comfortable) height and turn the lathe on to a slow setting. Use the equation on page 83 to ensure it isn't rotating too fast.

1

2

3

4. Begin cutting the bottom and outside walls of the bowl, following the cutting-action instructions outlined earlier in this section. Use the parting tool to create a recess or spigot in the bottom of the bowl, as shown here. When initially making contact with the wood, come in with low hands and the chisel pointing higher than the cutting point. Then move the chisel down slowly to find the cutting point: You'll know when you have found it, since the chisel will begin to cut and you will see curls of wood. Every time you come off the wood and then return to it, use this technique until you are sure you know exactly where the cutting point is.

5. Work up the grits, sanding the bottom of the bowl and the spigot / recess.

6. Take the bowl off the lathe with the faceplate. Unscrew the faceplate. Attach the chuck jaws to the spindle and then clamp the recess / spigot within the chuck jaws; tighten well.

7. Begin turning the hollow of the bowl, using the bowl gouges. You must remember to move the tool rest in as far as possible to give yourself the right support inside the hollow.

8. When happy with the hollow, begin to sand, working up through the grits until smooth.

6

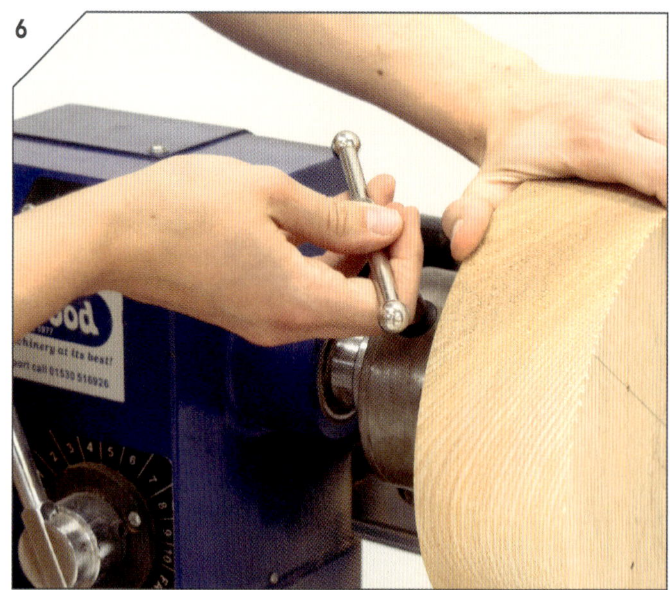

7

5

8

9. Decide on a finish for the bowl: milk paint, yakisugi, or simply oiling work well. It is easiest to apply milk paint and oil when the bowl is still on the lathe, since this means you can sand easily between coats. However, take the bowl off the lathe for a yakisugi finish.

Yakisugi

Translating from Japanese as "burnt cedar," yakisugi is also less commonly known (at least in the West) as *sho sugi ban*. In Japan, this technique has been used for centuries to char the wood cladding on buildings, especially around coastal areas. It is also used in traditional woodworking to add various preservation qualities, as well as giving a striking visual effect to the wood.

Although it appears counterintuitive, charring wood offers multiple amazing qualities, including water resistance, fire resistance, antibacterial properties, and the ability to repel pests. Because of these qualities, charring cladding creates a hard-wearing shell for any wooden building. However, yakisugi can be used in the interior of our homes, where its properties are especially brilliant in the kitchen for utensils, bowls, chopping boards, and so on.

As a passionate advocate for all natural finishes, I find yakisugi effective, since it circumvents the need to finish your work with oils or milk paints. After you are done charring the wood, the grain will have created its own condensed, resistant shell. However, when I use the item in the kitchen, I still like to do the same routine of a tung oil coat followed with natural wood wax.

Another benefit of charring is the durability it gives the wood. It can elongate the life span of the piece and, as a bonus, needs minimal upkeep. You can also use the yakisugi technique to suit your own aesthetic. I tend to do one pass of charring the wood before brushing, but some woodworkers like to char again and again, until the wood almost splits. I tend to avoid going this far, since with regular wear, these ridges can split and create weak spots in the wood, lessening its durability and life span.

Yakisugi Scoop

For centuries the Japanese have used yakisugi externally on buildings to char wood cladding. It ages well, changing color from black to silvery gray. But that's an external process caused by weathering: If the wood is sealed—housebuilders use polyurethane—the beautiful charred color lasts for much longer. You can achieve the same result indoors with a blowtorch, oil, and wax to create beautifully colored household utensils such as this sycamore spoon.

Materials:

Beeswax, blowtorch, mask, slate, tung oil, wax, wire brush, wire wool or steel wool, wooden spoon

1. First, choose a piece of wood to char. A great option for a yakisugi project is a chopping board, because that really benefits from having a hard-wearing, water- and bacteria-resistant finish. Other ideas include a yakisugi candle holder as a striking centerpiece for your table. The only thing to remember is not to char anything that is already treated with oil, since this will impact the effectiveness of the char. For this demonstration, I have chosen the sycamore scoop I carve in the Utensil section on page 114.

2. Select the chosen object, and, using a heat-resistant surface—I like to use a large piece of slate and work outside—put it on the ground or on an inflammable surface. Keep it well away from grass, leaves, or anything likely to catch fire within a few yards' radius of the blowtorch.

3. Turn on the blowtorch and char the piece one side at a time, being careful to leave it to cool between picking it up and turning it over to char the other side. Try not to hold the blowtorch on one area for too long. Keep the flame moving, and as soon as the area has turned a charcoal-black color, move on.

1

2

3

4. Once the piece is fully charred, ensure the blowtorch is securely off, stored upright, and left somewhere safe to cool down. Take the piece to a suitable location to be rubbed back. This process can be messy, since it loosens all the soot and removes it from the grain. I like to use a brass wire suede brush (essentially a very soft wire brush) and brush this over the wood, always moving along the length of the grain. Do this until almost no char comes off. Then remove the finer dust with a soft brush and move on to wire wool, getting finer and finer. The grain will reveal itself, and the deep charcoal finish will get slightly lighter, but don't panic; this will be brought back to a rich charcoal with oil.

4

5. When you have removed as much soot as possible, take the piece to the sink for a quick wash. It seems counterintuitive to hold your piece under a tap at this point, but the wood is well sealed, and this will not raise the grain as it would if it hadn't been charred. I use a small amount of very gentle detergent or hand soap to lightly wash the piece and remove all final excess soot.

6. Leave the piece to dry naturally; then it is ready to oil and wax. Using the technique previously described on pages 48–49, oil the piece and leave it to soak in for a couple of days before applying wax.

5

FUNCTIONAL DESIGN

This next chapter is a more in-depth selection of projects that call on the skills we have learned. These projects range from bound brushes to chopping boards and utensils for the kitchen, and all of them utilize the skills you have now become comfortable with. Pull sawing, filing, sanding, and finishing techniques are used in almost every project, so have these tools at the ready and refer back to their sections in the book if you need a reminder. All of these instructions are guides. The aim is not for you to make the exact same design that I am demonstrating (although that is fine, too), but to get creative to make the things you want in your own home.

Maybe you have a specific style in your home that you want to follow through in your projects. Perhaps you enjoy bold colors and want to paint all your pieces in a milk paint finish. The most important thing is to work to create something you enjoy looking at and using.

Ensuring that designs are functional plays a large role in these projects. If something is designed to work well, it means it will actually be used. In turn, this ensures the materials we make are cherished, not only for their aesthetic qualities but also for their durability and usefulness. A good way of making sure this is true of your own projects is to refer back to the Design for Utility section (page 14) before you begin anything. Write these questions down and answer each one in turn. This outline of functional design will help you create something that can be used every day, as well as admired and appreciated.

brush binding

The process of binding fibers is very meditative, almost trance-like in itself. Once you're comfortable with the dexterity of the technique, you can get creative with the shape, bristle material, and binding material to experiment with brushes for different uses. The binding can be done in multiple colors, and the steps can be added on different sides to create interesting shapes and different levels of firmness.

Materials:

Broomcorn fiber, hemp or nylon cord, rolling pin (or long, straight dowel), scissors, weighing scales

For this project I recommend using hemp, a biodegradable and natural cord. However, because hemp isn't very strong, use fibers no thinner than $^{1}/_{8}$ in. (3 mm). For something a little more hard-wearing, go instead for a $^{3}/_{32}$–$^{1}/_{8}$ in. (2 - or 3 mm) twisted nylon cord. Both are great options, but with different tensile strengths and benefits.

Hemp can be found in its natural color or already colored with natural dyes, so there is no chance of nasty lurking chemicals. However, as it is natural, you have to get used to the tensile strength of hemp and not pull quite as hard as you would with the same thickness of nylon. Nylon is a brilliant cord to use but is synthetic, so will not biodegrade; however, in terms of the brush's strength, it will last a lot longer and keep the tightness of the bind longer, making the end product a hard-wearing broom that will last many years.

For this project I used broomcorn fiber. It is incredibly hard-wearing, flexible, and water-resistant, so it is brilliant for use in brushes. It is a waxy fiber and can be bound in different ways to create a brush for hard floors, counter tops, workshops, or carpets, or for general tidying up in the garden.

You need only a few extra items to make a broom, the most important being a wooden foot break. This can take the form of a rolling pin, or just a short bit of chunky wooden dowel. The use for this becomes more apparent within the steps, but this piece of wood acts as an underfoot break to pull against when you want to add tension to the binding. And finally, you will need some scales to weigh out the fiber, and a pair of scissors to trim the cord and fiber at the end.

Brush binding is a technique that requires a full-body movement, so the first challenge is to make yourself comfortable and listen to your body while you work. I like a seat that allows my legs to sit at a 90 degree angle, with my feet flat on the floor and my foot break underneath. I always make sure I have a table nearby so I can reach my bundles of fiber while I work, without needing to move too much. Finally, before you start, make sure you have no shoes on, but put on some nice woolly socks. This will help protect your feet, as well as allow the foot break to turn easily without friction.

1. Measure out the cord for the brush and wrap the full length around the center of the foot break, leaving about a 20 in. (50 cm) tail. If you use 13.4 in. (34 cm) broomcorn as I did, measure out about 20 ft. (6 m) of cord. If your fiber is shorter or longer, you need slightly less or more—it's always better to have extra. Additionally, measure and cut a 20 in. (50 cm) length of cord and set it aside for later use, but keep it in arm's reach.

   Weigh the fiber. My 13.4 in. (34 cm) broomcorn fiber was 3 oz. (85 g)—a nice weight and thickness for this project. If using a shorter length—for example, something only 8 in. (20 cm) long—consider using a lower weight, possibly 2.5 oz. (70 g), since this will ensure that the brush isn't overly stiff and still has a nice fan on it.

2. Split the broomcorn into eight "step" piles by weight. Stack them in a X shape, alternating each direction so that the steps don't merge and are easy to pick up. Finally, take your top (eighth) pile and split it in half, giving half to the top step you will pick up first and half to the second step.

3. Find a comfortable position with your fiber pile within arm's reach and the foot break under your feet, with the 20 in. (50 cm) tail of cord threaded up to your knee. Tie a regular knot in the end of the cord about an inch (2 cm) from the end. Broomcorn has a top and bottom to the fiber, which you need to remember when picking up the piles. The bristle of the brush needs to be made from the fluffier end, where the seeds grew on the plant. The handle end is the stiffer and thicker end of the fiber.

1

2

3

4. Pick up the fiber with your dominant hand. I am left-handed, so I always pick up and add in fiber with my left hand while holding the brush with my right. It will take practice to figure out which way is comfortable for you. Once this is settled, pick up the top fiber step with your comfortable hand, hold the knot in the cord with the other, and use your thumb to bury the knot into the center of the step. I find it easiest to use my index finger and thumb of my other hand to close the fiber around the knot as it sinks in, then start rotating the fiber straight away.

4

5. When you start rotating, ensure your cord is spiraling up toward the top end of the fiber. I find that rotating my hands away from me is the most comfortable and natural direction to rotate. At the same time, let your feet relax as you pull the cord upward to bind, and then press down on your feet and pull upward with your hands every two or three rotations to apply extra tension to the cord. I like to do a minimum of five rotations before I think about adding another step. This ensures that the step is held well and that each step will be definitively visible in the finished design.

5

6. Adding the next step can feel a little daunting, since you must keep the tension on the cord at all times to make sure all that lovely tension you have put in doesn't unwind. The best way to do this is to put your thumb—whichever is easiest—on the end of the binding and press firmly to keep that tension in the binding, then pick up the second step. I like to give each step a little pat on the end, maybe on my knee or on the table, to make sure the fiber is nice and neat as it goes into the brush. Add the second step to the brush, making sure it sits covering the entrance of the cord into the fiber. Review the photographs to clearly understand the process before proceeding.

6

7. Begin rotating away from yourself again, remembering to keep the tension at all times. After rotating a step twice, I like to do a pinch and pull, which is to take the index finger and thumb of my non-dominant hand, and pinch the point where the second step starts to bind the new fibers together. With this pinched, pull a good amount of tension on the cord and prevent the second step merging into the first step. This makes the steps clearly visible.

8. Continue to bind, adding steps every five or so binds, whichever number you've chosen. I like to keep all my binding amounts the same on each step to get an even finish. Different-sized steps create different shapes in the brush, so feel free to experiment. When adding steps, always add the latest step onto the previously bound step to create the attractive laddering effect we are looking for.

9. After adding the final step, simply keep binding up the handle. The steps pushed the binding out flat and wide, but the fiber in the handle will naturally become rounded as you continue to bind. When you are about a third of the way up the handle, add the finishing loop. This is not part of the handle, but a loop that will allow us to bind the fiber back on itself once finished.

Choose which side will be the back of the brush, and take the pre-measured 20 in. (50 cm) length that was set aside at the beginning. Double this by overlaying it along the length of the handle, with the loop end pointing out from the top of the brush. Continue binding over this loop, ensuring that there's a good amount pointing down toward the bristles. Still pull tension from your foot break every two or three rotations.

10. Once you are two-thirds up the handle, it is time to start thinking about the handle itself. I like to make my handle out of the same piece of cord, since it is satisfying to know that this one piece of cord is unbroken and bound around the whole brush. Besides, I think it looks aesthetically better.

To do this, consider the way your steps move up the brush. (**10a**) Take your non-dominant-hand thumb and hold where the binding finishes in line with the step, pull a bit of slack from the foot break, and loop over the top of the brush, bringing the cord back down to the opposite side of the brush in line with the final step. (**10b**) Hold in place with the index finger of your non-dominant hand. With your dominant hand, wrap twice more around the end of the brush and then pull tension while you release your finger and thumb.

9

10a

10b

11a

11b

11c

11. Continue to bind until you have about an inch (2 cm) of fiber left at the top of the brush. This is where the binding finishes and the finishing loop comes into play. Holding tension with your non-dominant thumb, pull slack from the foot break and cut the cord (**11a**), giving yourself about a foot (30 cm) of length from the brush.

(**11b**) Still keeping the tension with your thumb, use your other hand to carefully thread the end line through the finishing loop.

(**11c**) Then use the two ends of the finishing loop to pull the end line down through the handle. It should reappear where you put the finishing loop in.

12. Trim the brush fibers at the top of the handle and at the base of the brush. Then trim the end line, which is still loose on the handle. Finally, prep your brush for sweeping with a good beat. I tend to use my arm, but you can use a table or chair side, and beat the bristles against it. You will release loose fiber and a bit of debris, but this just makes sure that the fibers are clean before the brush is used.

wooden utensils

Public perspective on using natural materials in the home has changed with the mass production of plastics, and the convenience and practicality of man-made materials. I get asked a lot of questions about the longevity and cleanliness of using wooden tools in the kitchen, since there is a common misconception that wooden items are unwashable and will perish quickly. Understanding the natural material and how to look after and use it means these items will, in fact, outlive us. Of course, when we buy wood over plastic, our priority isn't it lasting hundreds of years, but the knowledge that it will outlast us with no detriment to the environment. Moreover, if you can work with a priority of utilizing wooden offcuts that are not otherwise used, then you are saving that material from being discarded or burnt.

Materials:

Food-safe oil, files, milk paint (optional), sandpaper in various grits, saw, wooden offcuts (12 in. / 30 cm length); technical compass and carving chisels—including a spoon gouge—for the scoop

That leads us to what kind of wood to choose for this type of domestic project. If you're a novice woodworker, I suggest that rather than buying wood blanks to work from, you try first approaching any joiners in your area who may have offcuts on hand. I trained in joinery after my degree, and my eyes were opened to the amount of beautiful hardwoods that go to waste in larger joinery companies. Chances are, a joiner's workshop will have an offcut pile from which they will be happy for you to pick some pieces for a much-lower price than buying blanks. On top of that, they will most likely be lovely, seasoned hardwoods that are perfect for the small projects in this book. The reasonable but unhappy fact is that many offcuts are too small for professional joiners to use, so offcuts go to the burn pile, since they hold little or no value to a woodworker working on larger-scale pieces. However, this is where I find my purpose, in that this material has value and has spent years of time and resources growing. It deserves to be utilized.

Search out where to pick up hardwoods for these projects, since these are the woods that will last through a lifetime of use. For cooking or food preparation, look out for species such as sycamore, beech, or olive woods, since their grain is tight. In particular, the oils within olive help protect the wood from heat. Oak looks like a lovely option, but as these cooking utensils will get hot and be in contact with food, avoid it; oak releases tannins that can discolor food.

For this project you need a saw to cut the shape down and files to work it. The saw can be a hand saw—a pull saw. You could do the shaping with one file, but it's probably better to have a couple of differently shaped files available for different curves.

For finishing, an optional step to add some character to the utensil is to add some color in the form of milk paint. Just paint this on and sand between coats, or simply dip the handle into the milk paint to give it a lovely pop of color. Finally, you will need sandpaper and food-safe oil—I use tung oil to finish my utensils.

1. The first step is to find a suitable cut of wood and decide the shape of the utensil. Draw the shape on in pencil when you have worked out a plan. You can see that I have a good-sized offcut to work from, so I am utilizing as much of the wood as I can, with four designs arranged there.

1

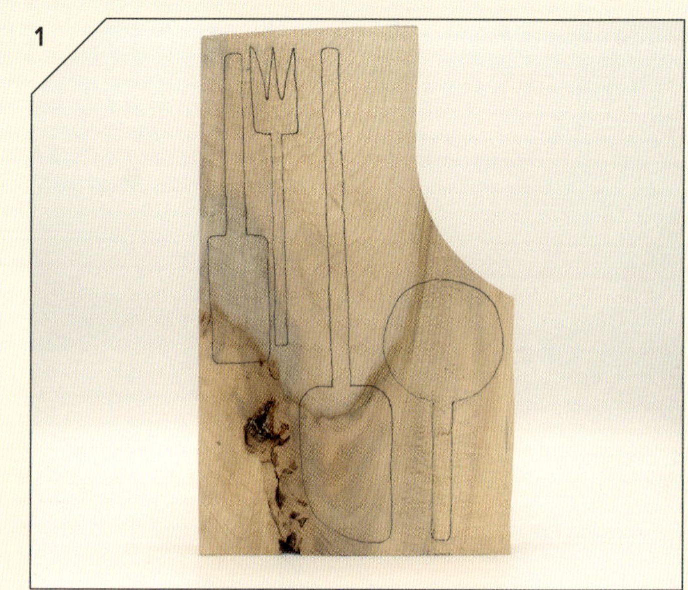

2. Once you have finalized your shapes, take a saw and cut as close to the pencil line as you can. If you're using a pull saw, this will be in the form of lots of small cuts, since pull saws cannot make curved lines. To cut a concave curve, see the technique for cutting and filing on page 39.

2

3. With the shape cut clean from the wood, it's time to finalize with a hand file. If you have access to a sander, use this to finalize the shape and finish of the wood. You could also add texture using smaller carving chisels or a carving knife.

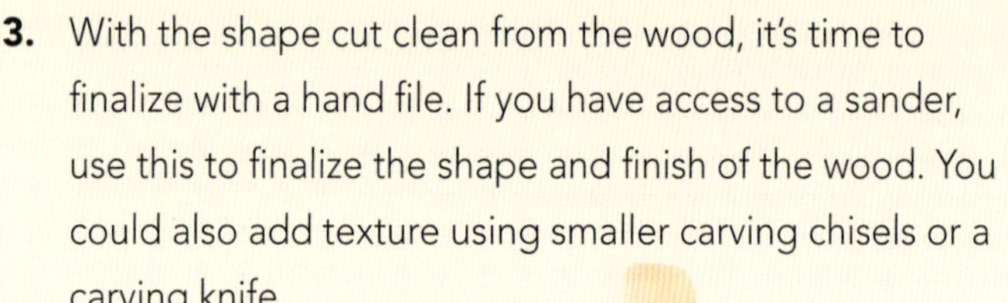

4. To finalize the finish, work up through the grits and give the utensil a thorough sanding all over. Since these utensils will be getting wet, it's a good idea to raise the grain a few times and sand it back. To do this, all you need is a rag or brush. Dampen it with water, then wipe it over the surface. Wait for the wood to dry; you will notice that as it dries, parts of the grain will rise and become rough. Sand this all back to the finish you want and then follow this process a few more times. The result will be that, when you're cooking, the grain will remain stable and retain a smooth finish.

5. Color is an entirely optional step, but adds character to the utensil and can create a lovely aesthetic in your kitchen. I suggest adding milk paint to the handle. Milk paint is a brilliant option for adding color to wood. It is water-based and soaks into the grain beautifully, without hiding the grain. It is also completely natural, food-safe, and chemical-free, so it can be used on anything around the home, including children's toys and cooking utensils.

   To mix milk paint, follow the instructions on the product you get, but it goes a long way, so mix only a spoonful at a time, especially for a small project like this. When the paint is mixed, you can either paint your color onto the handle or dip the handle into the paint and hang it up to dry. Since the paint is primarily decorative, avoid adding it to the end, which becomes hot and will contact food, since it will flake more easily.

6. Finally, finish and seal the wood with a food-safe oil. I like to use tung oil, since this is 100 percent food-safe, and as it soaks into the grain, it hardens the wood. This means it creates a strong barrier between the wooden utensil and all the heat, water, and acidity it will be coming into contact with.

4

5

6

Another handy kitchen utensil is a scoop, and to make one we need to hollow out the wood to create a scoop or spoon shape. To do this will require an additional set of carving chisels, and, specifically, a spoon-gouge carving chisel to create the inner hollow of the scoop. (Note: In practice, this piece would be clamped while being worked on; the clamp was omitted for photography purposes.)

1. Once you have your shape, cut as close to your design line as you can; it is time to clamp the scoop to the bench and pick up a technical compass. Draw a centralized circle on the side of the scoop you want to hollow. This will give a carving guide to work around.

2. Standing with your feet shoulder-width apart and one in front of the other, work with the direction of grain wherever you can. Begin to carve the hollow of the spoon: This can be quite tough, since we are working with dried, hard timber. It is important always to push the blade of the gouge away from yourself. Move your body or work accordingly to ensure you never push the chisel with force toward your body.

1

2

3. Use a mallet if you need to help the chisel cut through the wood. Using a mallet will create more-forceful cuts, so if you begin using one, stop as soon as you come close to finishing cuts. Abandon the mallet and just use your hands to get a smoother cut.

4. As you progress, you will start to see where you need to shape more. Try to keep the sides of your scoop a nice thickness to ensure it is sturdy and proportional.

5. Once the scoop has been hollowed, it is time to shape the handle, as well as the outside and inside of the scoop, more finely. Finish following the technique described in steps 3 and 4, refining as you go.

3

4

wood-handled brush with wire-drawn setting

Setting bristles into wooden handles is another historical technique by which hard-wearing and long-lasting brushes are created. Common practice dates the craft back to eighteenth-century Europe. Wire-drawn setting essentially means stitching the bristles into a handle with wire. The result is long-lasting and more sustainable than using chemical-based adhesives. Glues have their place in brushmaking, but I always advise using PVA-based glues, since these are lower in toxicity than other adhesives.

Materials:

Wooden offcuts / saws / files / finish of your choice to create the handle; arenga / tampico / coir fiber, copper / brass / galvanized steel wire, drill and drill bits ($^5/_{16}$ in. / 8 mm, $^5/_{64}$ in. / 2 mm) for the bristles and setting.

The brushes we make in this chapter are multipurpose, meant for use around the home or in the garden. Deciding what type of wire to use depends on the intended work for the brush. If it's to be used outdoors or somewhere that will get wet often, it's sensible to go with a galvanized steel wire, since this holds tension well and is resistant to corrosion.

However, if you want to match an aesthetic, or have an indoor brush for use around a hearth—for example, a dusting brush, or crumb brush—using a lovely brass or copper wire adds a special touch. These wires are slightly more flexible, so they can release tension with vigorous use, but for gentle use around the home they're perfect.

If you choose to use a galvanized steel or brass wire, look for 20 AWG (American Wire Gauge). If you want to use copper, ideally find a copper-plated steel wire at 18 AWG, since copper is too soft to be used as pure wire.

Choosing the bristle on your brush can be another difficult choice, but some good natural options are as follows:

Arenga Brown/black in color. Ideal for making a hearth brush or potting brush.

Coir Caramel in color. Useful for softer dusting and sweeping on hard surfaces.

Tampico Light yellow in color. Great for fine dusting, and as a table or crumb brush.

All of these fibers are water-resistant and don't rot easily, meaning they can be rinsed and dried between uses if need be. For this project, the fiber needs to be twice as long as the finished brush fiber length, so ensure you order fiber that is over double the length you want in the head of your brush.

Your choice of wood is ultimately based on aesthetics with this project. I like to use all of my offcut-sourced wood well, so if you think you have a piece that will lend itself to this project, go for that one. Spalted wood adds a beautiful aesthetic to a brush, but you can also think about using yakisugi to create a lovely charred finish—this will really make your copper or brass wire stand out in comparison.

Spalted beech hand brush with brass wire setting and coir fiber. This brush and others like it are available at www.function-and-form.com.

1. Start by prepping the brush handle. This comes down to choosing the wood, shape, finish, and, finally, how the bristles are going to set into the handle. Because the bristles are stitched into the brush, think about the entrance and exit of the wire. Both of these surfaces are easier to drill and stitch if they're flat, so keep that in mind when deciding on the shape of the brush. You may decide you would like something more natural-looking, and for this project, it's completely fine to find some fallen branches and choose something with a nice thickness as the handle.

2. With the shape of the handle decided, it's time to cut it to shape and finish it. This can be done using the pull saw and various files. Use the yakisugi technique to give a beautiful charcoal effect, or simply oil the handle and let that soak in for a couple of days. Another option is milk paint—the choice is all yours!

3. Once your handle is finished and oiled, it's time to think about drilling the holes for the brush fibers and wire stitching. This wire stitching threads through the top side, and the bristles emerge from the bottom side. The first decision is to choose the top of the handle, then measure and mark out the fiber holes. I like to ensure there is at least $^1/_5$ in. (5 mm) between the edges of my drilled holes.

1

2

3

4. Drill with a hand drill or pillar drill and a $^{5}/_{64}$ in. (2 mm) bit, down into the top side of the brush and all the way through the wood. Next, drill with a $^{5}/_{16}$ in. (8 mm) bit from the bottom side, but only halfway through the handle, so that from the bottom, you see a $^{5}/_{16}$ in. (8 mm) hole and at the top you see the $^{5}/_{64}$ in. (2 mm) hole. This is because the bristles will spread themselves into the larger holes, and the wire will pull up and through the smaller holes at the top.

5. Separate out the bundles of fiber into workable amounts so you can easily pick up as you go. When building the bundles, remember that they will halve as they go into the setting, so assemble bundles that will be enough to double up in each hole. Collect sufficient bundles to fill each setting.

6. After drilling, check for any wood chips and dust left inside the holes: These can stop the fibers from setting properly. Begin to stitch with the wire. Starting and finishing the wire setting is important, since this is what keeps the tension in the bristles.

   Beginning at the top end of the brush, take the wire and thread it through the small hole down and out through the large hole. This way the brush handle is threaded onto the wire. Next, take the first bundle of fiber and wrap the end of the wire around the half-way point once, then twist the end around itself so that it holds the fiber tightly together. Pull the wire back down through the handle, using pliers or a vise, pulling firmly until you feel the halved bundle sink into place in the setting. Study the photographs for a clear visual explanation of the process.

4

5

6

7. Now you should have the first bundle in place, and the wire should be poking up out through the top of the handle. Thread the wire back down through the next hole and place your fiber bundle through the loop at the half-way point as before.

8. Pull the wire back up through the hole and set the next bundle firmly in place. If you find that the wire is struggling to lie flat on the back of the handle, take a soft mallet and give the wire a gentle tap to set it flat against the wood. Repeat steps 7 and 8 through all the holes in the handle. (8b)

7

8a

8b

9. After threading the final bundle, when the wire has been pulled through the back of the handle, I like to pull the last fiber bundle slightly out of place and, while holding firmly on to the wire with pliers, twist the bundle so that the wire twists itself secure in the setting hole. After twisting a few times, pull the bundle back into place and cut the wire, leaving an extra 0.2 in. (5 mm) outside the hole. Fold this short piece of wire back on itself, trying to loop it over the wire that enters the hole. Give this a tap with a mallet to bury it in the hole and keep it secured in on itself.

10. The penultimate step is to give your brush a good thwack. I usually use my hand to whack the brush against something solid to release any loose fibers. This way, any fibers not caught in the stitch should come out before the brush is used. The last step is to trim the brush down to a nice flat edge.

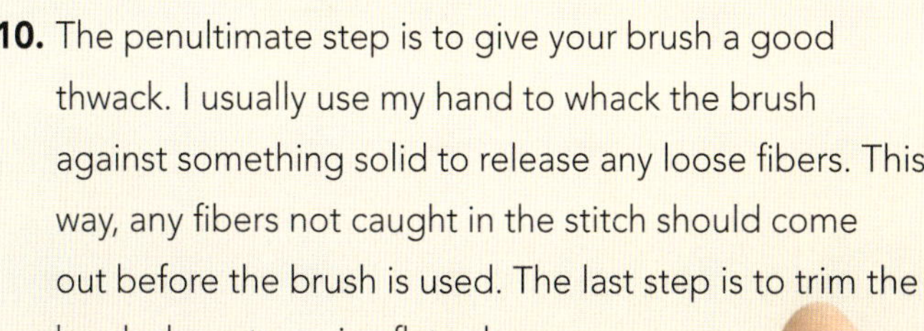

bud vase

Bringing the outdoors inside always makes a home feel more alive. I like to use dried stems to create features around the home, since these are not only a lot less maintenance than live flowers, but last a long time. This also means the live flowers can remain outside for pollinators to enjoy. Picking decorative dried seed heads from plants such as poppies, honesty (money plant), and various grasses gives a beautiful alternative to live flowers.

Materials:

Option 1. Carving chisels, drill and drill bits, file, sandpaper, saw, wooden offcuts; finishing material of your choice

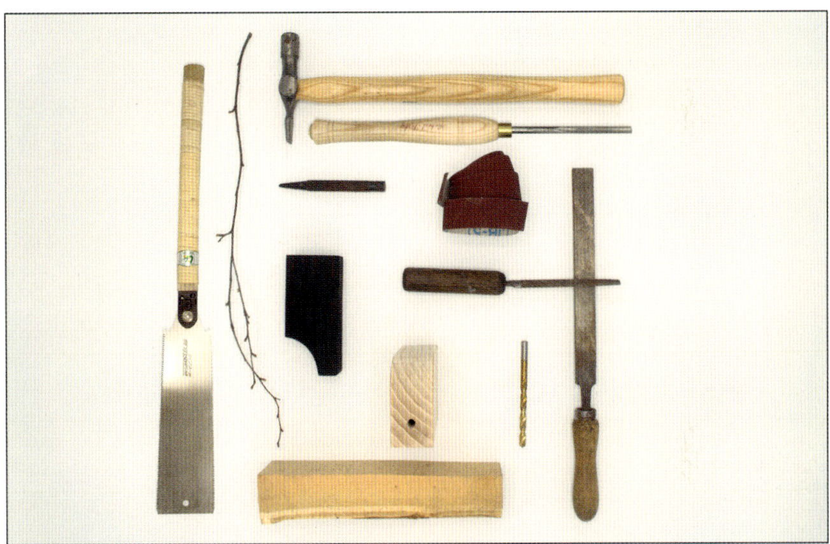

Option 2. Chuck jaws, lathe, prong drive center, ruler, sandpaper, tailstock center, tailstock drill chuck, turning chisels, wooden offcuts

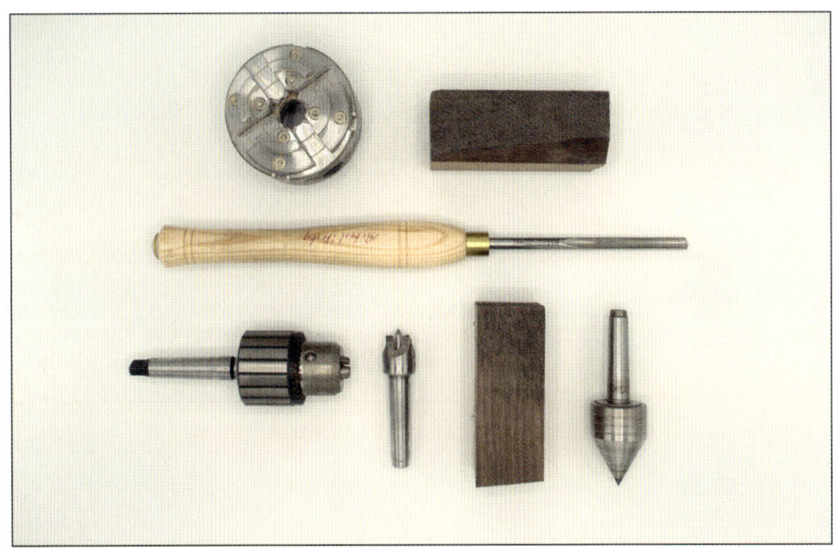

Option 1

I like to create simple little bud vases to hold a few stylish stems. They are very easy to make and have so much creative freedom about them. Similarly, a larger multi-stem holder can be created by adding more holes to the piece. There are many creative choices when it comes to how to make your piece: You can use only hand tools, or, if you have a lathe you've been dying to get started on, this is a perfect opportunity to learn all the beginner techniques a lathe can offer.

Learning how to work on the lathe is a very enjoyable process that allows you to form wood into the final design very quickly. A lathe predominantly creates things that are rounded in shape; think chair legs, broom handles, bowls, pestle and mortars, handles, plates … you get the idea! They are great fun to use once you fully understand all the safety precautions.

Picking the wood and design for this project is completely your choice. If planning on turning the piece, you need wood that is as wide as it is thick, since you will be cutting down to the smallest thickness. Another important aspect is the grain direction, especially if you are turning. You need the grain to run horizontally when it is attached to the lathe. So, in this case, ensure the wood has enough length in it for your intended design.

If you are doing this project with hand tools, continue with option 1. To learn how to complete this on the lathe (option 2), refer to step 1 on page 138.

1. Choose your piece of wood and the design you like for it. A slightly thicker piece of wood lends itself nicely to being shaped into a bud vase design. If you have a piece with a natural or wavy edge on it, you might like to work with this feature in the final design. Once decided on a design, draw the shape you want onto the wood with a pencil, and start cutting.

2. Cutting out can be done with a hand saw. Note also that slightly thicker pieces—such as those illustrated—are best held securely in a vise or with clamps when hand cutting. Use your saw of choice to cut as close to the design line as you can. To cut a concave curve, see the technique for cutting and filing on page 39.

3. While you still have a flat bottom on the design, drill where you want your stems to sit. Drilling an appropriate hole depends on whether you want it to hold multiple stems or just one. For a single stem, I suggest a hole about 0.2 in. (4 mm) in diameter; for multiple-stem vases, you can go up to 0.3–0.4 in. (8–10 mm) diameter.

4. Shaping can be done in multiple ways. If looking for a final smooth finish, use a file to sand the piece down to its final shape. For a more textured finish, use a chisel and cut texture into the surface of the shape. Alternatively, yakisugi gives a striking charcoal finish. Stay aware of how you want your bud vase to sit, since it needs a flat bottom to be stable.

Finishing the bud vase depends on the technique you choose. For a smooth finish, continue to sand up the grits. If you have a chiseled, textured finish, use very high-grit sandpaper to smooth off rough edges between cuts. When using yakisugi, refer back to pages 98–99 for the finishing technique. You don't necessarily need to oil the bud vases if you don't want to, since they won't be coming into contact with something they need to be sealed for. I have left mine with their natural finish and a yakisugi finish without oiling.

1

2

3

4

Option 2

1. The first step is to choose your wood. Remember that, when using a lathe, the wood needs to be as thick as it is wide; this way, you make the most of the material. Most seasoned hardwoods are lovely to turn, but some are harder to work with than others. Beech is a lovely wood to work, as are lime (or basswood) and sycamore.

   For this option you will also need turning chisels on hand, as well as the chuck jaws, the tailstock center, and the tailstock drill chuck.

2. Using a ruler and pencil, go from one corner of the end grain to the opposite corner to find the center of your wood on both ends. Using the prong drive center (clamped into the chuck jaws) and the tailstock center, clamp the wood into the lathe, ensuring that the centers are in contact with the wood where the lines cross on both ends.

1

2

3. Move the tool rest to about halfway up the piece of wood and tighten it. Start the lathe on a lower speed setting and pick up the larger roughing gouge. If you have turned before, use the technique that suits you best. If you are new to turning, ensure your feet are well placed to give balance and ease of moving away quickly. Your chisel hand (usually the left hand) should be used to push the chisel down onto the tool rest, while your other hand (usually the right hand) is at the bottom of the chisel handle and guides the chisel right and left, up and down.

4. When initially making contact with the wood, come in with low hands and the chisel pointing higher than the cutting point. Then move the chisel down slowly to find the cutting point: You'll know when you have found it, since the chisel will begin to cut and you will see curls of wood. Every time you come off the wood and then return to it, use this technique until you are sure you know exactly where the cutting point is.

3

4

5. Once in contact with the wood, begin to move the chisel left and right, being careful not to fall off the end of the tool rest, since this can cause the chisel to catch on your chucks and damage them. Carry on using your largest gouge until you have a smooth cylinder. From time to time while taking this material off, you will need to stop the lathe and move the tool rest closer to the wood, always ensuring there is no more than about a 0.2–0.4 in. (5–10 mm) gap between the wood and the tool rest. Stop the lathe every so often and check if there are any flat surfaces left on the wood. You can tell that the wood is cylindrical when you stop feeling vibrations on the chisel.

6. Using the parting tool, create a foot at the headstock end of the wood with about 0.4 in. (10 mm) width. The foot needs to be small enough to be clamped into the chuck jaws.

5

6

7. Once the wood is cylindrical and the foot is carved in, take it off your lathe and remove the prong drive center from the chuck jaw. Now clamp the wooden foot straight into the jaw chuck. I use my tailstock center to help center the piece at that end as I clamp it into the jaw chuck.

8. When fully secure and clamped in (tighten the jaws well), take the tailstock center away and attach the drill chuck to the tailstock. Then insert and tighten the chosen drill bit into the drill chuck.

9. Move and secure the tailstock so that the drill bit is about 0.1 in. (2 mm) from the end of the piece of wood. Turn the lathe onto a slow setting and begin to use the handwheel at the end of the tailstock to press the drill bit into the end of your piece. Reverse it out when you're done, turn off the lathe, remove the drill chuck, and replace it with the tailstock center again.

8

7

9

10. Clamp the tailstock center back into the hole just created for the vase, and start the lathe. You can start to turn the speed up a little now as the shaping and finishing process begins. Design the final shape of the vase, utilizing the chisels you have. Always remember to go in steady with the chisels and never force them: Your chisels should be sharp enough to cut without being pushed hard into the wood. Make an incision near the chuck jaws to mark where the bottom of the vase will be.

11. When happy with your final design, it's time to sand. Before you make contact with the surface of the wood, ensure you have taken off any sharp corners first, since wooden corners can be deceptively sharp. Sanding on the lathe feels a lot quicker than hand sanding, since you hold the sandpaper on the wood and the lathe does the rest. Always remember to start with a lower grit and work your way up for a nice, clean finish.

10

11

12

12. With the work finally shaped and sanded, it is time to oil the bud vase. Do this while it is still on the lathe. Spin the piece as you hold the oil rag up to it.

13. Now part the piece off the lathe. You can do this on the lathe with a parting tool, which you slowly push through the wood at the point where you made the base until the piece is separated from the wood in the chuck jaws. The other option is to take the wood off the lathe and cut the piece with a hand saw at the point you marked as the base.

13

chopping board

Every kitchen needs one—even if you're a basic chef! Creating a chopping board for your home is also one of the most simple DIYs out there, and you need very few tools to complete the project. Chopping boards went through an overhaul recently, following widespread misinformation about the poor hygiene issues surrounding wooden chopping boards. Interestingly, this has been completely disproven, and in fact the opposite proved: that wood is actually antibacterial. As bacteria come into contact with wood grain, they are absorbed by the grain and die.

The ultimate chopping board is an end-grain board. These are commonly called butcher's blocks, and as such have been used by butchers for their robustness and ability to withstand daily, vigorous use. They are self-healing and will keep the knife edge sharp. Once you have mastered the techniques in this section, you may feel bold enough to move on to experiment with an end-grain board.

Materials:

Hand plane, sandpaper, saw, tung oil, wood wax (food safe), wooden offcut (planed, and as large as you want the board to be)

Carefully considering which wood to use for your chopping boards makes a big difference to their life span, and their ease of use and cleaning. Sycamore and beech are tight-grained hardwoods, and for an item that will be washed a lot, this is ideal. Tightness of grain also makes a difference when chopping strong-smelling foods such as onion and garlic: These smells are less likely to be absorbed into wood with a tighter grain.

Taking good care of the chopping board once it is made is another big factor for lifespan and ease of use. Ideally the wood needs to be sealed as thoroughly as possible once it's finished, to give it a good start. I like to use tung oil on all my items, even those that will not come into contact with food.

I finish my chopping boards with wax as a final layer to ensure a watertight seal. I like to make my own wood wax: My simple recipe is 70 percent tung oil to 30 percent natural (ideally local) beeswax. The method is to melt natural beeswax into a bain-marie. Add in tung oil and mix well. Pour out to set in a tin.

Never fully submerge wooden chopping boards, leave them to soak, or put them in a dishwasher, since this will immediately damage the wood. Instead, if you have smells in the board you want to get rid of, use salt and half a lemon and rub the salt into the board with the lemon half, allowing the juice to squeeze out as you work. Aside from this, wipe down the board with dish soap and a warm damp cloth. This does everything necessary—and, as said earlier, wood is antibacterial all on its own, so we don't need to do too much more. Finally, remember to oil your chopping board about once every six months if it's in daily use. You can also give it a light sand before oiling if you feel it's needed. This care will ensure the board lives a long life and will serve you and your family well for many years.

1. It's possible to discover wood for a chopping board in an offcut pile; otherwise, buy some FSC-certified timber to create exactly what you're looking for. As I mentioned above, it's important to get the right close-grained species of wood for your chopping board to ensure durability and ease of use. So if this means buying timber, the best course of action may be to go to a timber yard and ask for their planed wood. Some yards will have a selection of differing thicknesses and widths that you can look through. They can also be helpful with advice about which species to use.

2. Once you have found your piece of wood, it's time to think about shape and design. Since a chopping board will likely be used daily, also think about the weight of the board—you don't want it so large that it is challenging to handle. On the same point, it's good to think about how to hold the board: Will it have a handle? How will the handle fit the design?

3. When you have drawn the design on the board, it's time to put your pull-saw technique to the test. Cut the piece as close to the line as you can accurately cut. If there are any curves in the design, you may have to go carefully and finish these later with a file or sandpaper.

1

2

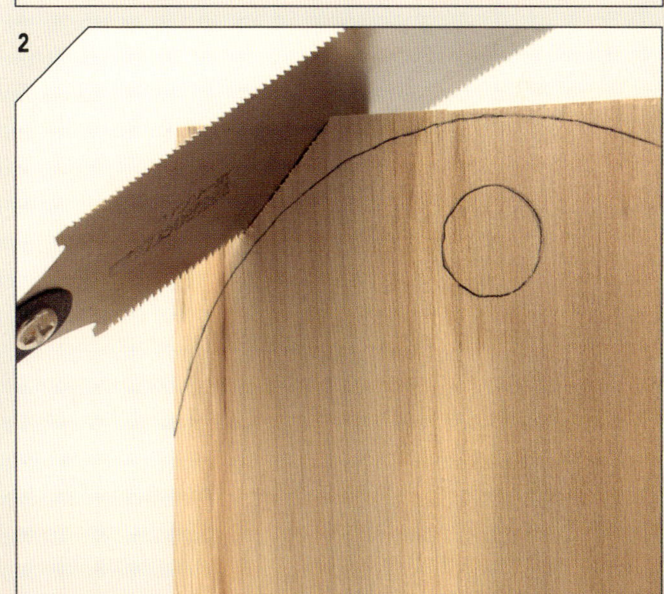

3

4. Next step is chamfering the edge of the board. To do this, use the hand plane and, utilizing your new skills, give the board a nice chamfer on all the edges, remembering to go inward when working on end grain.

5. A hanging loop is always a useful addition to a chopping board. You may have already worked this into your design, but you should think about how your chopping board will hang before you start. If the board is going to sit flat on the countertop, you want to ensure that the hanging loop doesn't in the way of the chopping board when lying flat. A simple way to create a hanging loop is to drill a largish hole in the board, so you can hang the board on a hook in the kitchen. To do this, you need a drill with a bit in the appropriate size.

6. Since the board will be coming into contact with water, it is best to raise the grain a few times. To do this, get a brush or rag and wipe water over the surface of the wood, covering it all over. As the water dries, it will raise the grain, which essentially expands any fibers that may be prone to expanding in contact with moisture. Once the water has dried, sand back again, working up the grits. You can do this as many times as you need, but I suggest a minimum of two. Then the finish will go on smoothly.

7. The board will look different depending on the finish you choose. Oil and wax or the yakisugi technique: I like a charred board, since this ensures a water-resistant and stable chopping board. For this project, I oiled and waxed my board with my homemade wax (recipe on page 148).

Before waxing, I like to put on a good coat of tung oil and then leave it to penetrate the board for a few days or even weeks, depending on the soak. My method is to really drench the board and leave it upright, so air can circulate for at least a couple of days before I wax. To wax the board, take an old lint-free cloth and rub the wax into the board, ensuring that all the surfaces are thoroughly coated.

GLOSSARY

against the grain: Working against the direction that the wood grain flows.

angle finder: *See* set square.

binding: The action of wrapping fibers in cord to create the structure of a bound broom.

blowtorch: Flame-producing tool, powered by a gas canister. Portable and refillable.

chamfer: A cut along a 90-degree edge of the material to take it down to a symmetrical and sloping edge.

character: Used to describe any kind of difference in grain which is not straight. Different species of timber lend themselves to different types of character (e.g. rippling in sycamore or pippy oak).

clamps: Come in all shapes and sizes. Clamps securely hold the material to another surface to give it stability.

countersink: Used after piloting the hole to allow the screwhead to sit flush with the surface of the timber.

crosscut: A cut that severs lengths of fibers across the direction of grain.

drill bit: A cutting tool used in the drill to create holes in material.

drive bit: An attachment to the drill that drives screws and fixings into material. The ends have differing heads to fit the type of fixing used.

eggbeater drill: An old-fashioned drill that rotates via a hand-powered crank.

end grain: The grain visible at the end of a plank of wood: A crosscut exposes end grain.

edge grain: Fibers of wood exposed in their full length and (depending on the way the timber has been sawn) usually has visibly straight fibers running the length of the edge. Can run slightly diagonally.

face grain: Fibers of wood exposed in their full length, and (depending on the way the timber has been sawn) usually shows irregular patterns as the growth rings intercept the surface.

fan: The bristle end of a brush created by combining steps.

file: Hand tool made from hardened steel, with fine rows of teeth used to scrape away fine layers of wood.

FFP1, 2, 3 rating: These ratings help identify what a mask will filter out, with FFP1 being the lowest level of filtration and FFP3 being the highest (N99 US equivalent for FFP3).

G-clamp: Versatile tool with a C- or G-shaped frame used to hold workpieces together firmly during tasks like gluing, welding, or drilling.

grain: The wood fiber that runs in the direction of growth of the tree.

hand drill: A battery or corded hand tool that allows you to drill holes or drive screws and fixings into wood.

hardwood: Word used to describe timber that comes from deciduous trees. Hardwoods are hard-wearing and dense and take a long time to grow.

knot: Occurs in timber where a branch has grown from the tree. The knot marks the point where the branch grew out.

mallet: Heavy, wooden hammer with a large head, used for adding more pressure to the top of carving chisels.

pilot hole: A preparatory hole drilled in advance of a screw or nail to guide and allow the fixing cleaner access.

plane: See box opposite.

PPE: Personal protective equipment.

pull saw: A traditional Japanese woodworking saw also known as nokogiri, which cuts on the pull stroke rather than the push stroke.

Plane

body: Main body of the plane.

depth adjusting nut: Located at the heel of a hand plane. Allows control of the depth the blade protrudes from the mouth, and therefore the depth of the cut.

heel: The back of the plane, which faces you when holding.

mouth: The opening in the sole of the plane where the blade protrudes.

sole: The bottom, flat face of the plane, which comes in contact with the wood.

toe: The front of the plane, which has contact with the wood first.

throat: Just above the mouth, where shavings exit from.

rip cut: This cut goes between the lengths of fiber with the direction of the grain.

ryoba: A double-sided saw that tends to have a crosscut blade on one side and rip-cut blade on the other. A great general hand saw.

saw: A hand or electric tool created for cutting through timber and other materials. Usually has a flat blade and a row of sharpened teeth, which are worked backward and forward to cut.

sanding: Utilizing sandpaper at varying grits to smooth the surface of a material.

sanding block: A rectangular block that holds sandpaper flat for sanding.

sandpaper: A roughened paper surface that, when pushed along the grain, removes material. Sandpaper is categorized by number and begins at lower numbers (40, 60), all the way up to high numbers (320, 600).

set square: Has a 90-degree angle guide used to find square on work. An angle finder is an alternative.

softwood: Word used to describe timber that comes from coniferous trees. Softwoods tend to be straight-grained and faster growing, but softer.

spoon gouge carving chisel: A chisel with a rounded end, suited to hollowing out the inside of scoops or spoons.

steel rule: Steel rulers are ideal for woodworking, since they have sharper, more-precise lines than plastic rulers.

steps: Individual bound bundles that come together to create the fan of a brush.

tear-out: The tearing of grain when cut in the wrong direction, or made inadvertently with a blunt blade.

technical compass: A tool used to draw circles or arcs from a given center point.

turning: See box on p. 156.

vise: Mechanical apparatus mounted on a work bench that has two parallel jaws that securely hold a workpiece for tasks such as drilling, sawing, or filing.

wire brush: Similar to a suede brush.

wire drawn setting: Drawing bristles into the handle of a broom using wire at the halfway point of the fiber.

wire wool: Also known as steel wool. Comes in differing grades. Used as an abrasive and for removing the ash from a yakisugi surface without removing the char.

with the grain: Working in the direction that the grain flows.

yakisugi: Traditional Japanese technique of sealing wood by charring it.

Turning

bed: Cast iron or steel rails running horizontally at the base of the lathe.

blank: A piece of wood specifically cut to size, ready for turning.

bowl gouges: These come in many shapes and sizes, all with fluted ends for hollowing and shaping the insides of bowls, plates, and cups.

chuck jaws: Usually three or four dovetail jaws to attach to the spindle and allow work to be attached to the lathe.

chisels: Made from HSS (high-speed steel) and have a variety of shapes for different cuts on the lathe.

flute: The long groove on gouge chisels.

gears: Change the speed that the spindle turns. Accessible by an adjustment knob or manually in the housing of the motor (for older models).

headstock: Houses the spindle, gears, and motor and location for on/off switch.

motor: Housed at the back of the lathe and sends power to the headstock to turn the spindle.

parting tool: A single-point chisel to create marks in work for referencing, or to completely separate material off the lathe.

pole lathe: Foot-powered lathe able to spin in both directions; used to turn green wood.

prong drive center: Attaches to the headstock and gives a centralized spike to clamp your piece in with. Used with the tailstock center to clamp the piece between the two.

recess: A hollowed-out area that allows the chuck jaws to clamp outward and hold the work.

roughing gouge: Large, fluted chisel used for roughing out material, cutting through waste material, and preparing forms to be shaped.

roughing out: Using the roughing gouge to take all the rough material off wood, leaving a smooth, finished surface to work into your form.

skew: A type of chisel often used in spindle turning. For making smooth cuts in the material, referred to as planing cuts.

spigot: Protruding section that allows the chuck jaws to clamp onto and hold work.

spindle: The protruding head at the headstock of the lathe to which the chucks and face plate are attached. Powered by the motor and controlled by the gears, it rotates the material.

spindle gouges: Similar to bowl gouges but with a more delicate and shallow-fluted end.

tailstock: At the opposite end of the lathe to the headstock. Can be used for supporting the free end of work or also used to drill holes using a tailstock drill chuck. Able to be moved up and down the bed to fit the work's length.

tailstock center: Cone-like spike that pushes into the tailstock to give central support to the end of a piece.

tailstock drill chuck: A lathe attachment that pushes into the tailstock with a drill attachment. Allows the drilling of centralized holes in your piece.

tool rest: A movable and adjustable rest that the user places the chisels on while turning.

TROUBLESHOOTING

Bound Brush

- If you are struggling with the hanging-handle step, you can always add in another piece of cord as the handle. This also makes for a nice design feature if you use a different color of cord.
- If you want to use the brush for a specific task, consider fewer steps for a narrower and firmer brush. If you add more steps, your fan elongates and becomes a softer sweeping brush.
- Consider experimenting with other fibers. The choice includes arenga, bassine, broomcorn, coco, or sisal. You can also make brushes with a mixture of fibers.

Chopping Board

- If you are not comfortable with a hand plane to chamfer the edges, or if you would like rounded edges, use a file to create the silhouette you like, then finish with sandpaper, working up the grits.

Fibers & Binding

- If you are struggling with the dexterity needed to keep your feet and hands working at the right times, try slowing everything down and start with just binding a simple one- or two-step-sized brush, and do this until it starts to become muscle memory.
- Try different positions for binding. Some people prefer to sit with their foot break under their feet; others find it more comfortable and controllable to stand while they bind, although this can become tiring after a while.

Hand Plane

- If your plane is jumping and creating small ripples on the work, chances are your blade is protruding too far from the mouth of the plane. This means it is trying to cut a lot of wood and can't get through it all.
- Sharpen your blade. You can do this in multiple ways; if you have a stone wheel sharpener, use the straight blade attachment and set the angle to 25 degrees and run the blade evenly back and forth until the whole blade is straight and smooth. Then, using your strop wheel and a small amount of metal polish, take the burr off the underside of the blade and polish along the top edge of the blade. Alternatively, use a sharpening block and water trough to sharpen the planer blades.
- When creating a chamfer, plane along the grain first while counting the passes. Then when you come to planing the end grain, go the full length across the end grain toward the face you have planed, until you reach the original amount of passes—corner wood should not catch, since it has been planed down.

Pull Saw

- If you are using a rip-cut blade to cut with the grain and you find it is jumping too much, try starting off the cut with the crosscut blade instead. The teeth are smaller and help the blade settle into cutting. Once the first few cuts are made, you can switch back to the rip-cut blade.
- When making your way through a piece of wood, the sound will start to change as you approach the underside. Listen for this, and, as the blade makes a lower-pitched sound, slow your cuts to ensure you don't tear out at the bottom, especially if you are crosscutting the grain.
- If you find your saw is binding—which you will notice if the blade stops mid-cut and your force creates a bend in the blade—try again, but put a lot less pressure on the saw. Let the saw's weight and the sharpness of the blade do the cutting.

Turning

- Always start the lathe on a slow gear, especially if you have a lot of material to rough out.
- Set the tool rest so it doesn't catch on your piece before you turn the lathe on.
- If your chisels are jumping, move the tool rest closer to your piece and check the angle of the chisels.
- If you are getting tear-out, sharpen your chisels and

check the tool rest height.

- If getting vibration on the wood, even though you know it has been planed, check that your centers at each end are still in place and clamped tightly.

Wire-Drawn Brush

- When drilling holes: If you don't have a workbench to drill down onto, use a scrap piece of wood under your brush handle to ensure your drill doesn't damage the surface underneath.
- If you are struggling with pulling enough tension on the wire, try using a vise to hold the brush in, then use pliers to pull the wire tight.
- You can wash the bristles of the brush, but try not to get the stitching wet.

Wooden Utensil

- Since these pieces will be getting washed regularly, remember to oil them every six months. Always handwash wooden utensils and never leave them soaking in the bowl or put them in the dishwasher.
- Once you are comfortable with the process, experiment by making multiple shapes and sizes for different uses around the kitchen.

Yakisugi

- Get experimental with how far you char the wood, but remember, if you char heavily on any corners, they will round and lose definition.
- Oiling and waxing isn't essential as it is with natural wood, so experiment with oiling the work or let its charcoal finish be the final look.
- The more open the grain, the more texture will be revealed after charring. If looking for a smooth finish, go for a tight-grained hardwood such as sycamore or beech. If looking for a textured piece, use woods such as ash or oak.